ANNUAL TAX MESS ORGANIZER

FOR

BARBERS, HAIR STYLISTS &

SALON OWNERS

By

KiKi Canniff

Published by
ONE MORE PRESS
P.O. Box 21582
Keizer, OR 97307
www.OneMorePress.com

Legal Disclaimer

The information in this book was published for the purpose of providing tax education to U.S. taxpayers and small business owners, and not for providing accounting or legal advice. The author does not make express or implied warranties in regard to the use of the enclosed information.

Cover Design

All One More Press book covers are the creation of the Northwest Publishers Consortium located in Lake Oswego, OR. (503)697-7964

ISBN: 978-0-941361-705

TABLE OF CONTENTS

ANNUAL TAX MESS ORGANIZER
FOR
BARBERS, HAIR STYLISTS &
SALON OWNERS

HOW THIS ORGANIZER WORKS

This Annual Tax Mess Organizer is for self-employed barbers, hair stylists and salon owners who are looking for a once-a-year bookkeeping system that will satisfy IRS tax needs while eliminating monthly recordkeeping headaches. This system requires no computer or special math skills.

This book is part of a series of Annual Tax Mess Organizers written for self-employed people. There is a basic volume (which will work for any profession) as well as seven industry-specific volumes in this series. All are perfect for small business owners who have not kept itemized income and expense records as the year went along.

Industry-specific Tax Mess Organizers are available for the following industries:

Barbers, Hair Stylists & Salon Owners
Independent Building Trade Contractors
Massage Therapists, Estheticians & Spas
Nail Techs, Manicurists & Salon Owners
Sales Consultants & Home Party Sales Reps
The Cannabis/Marijuana Industry
Writers, Artists, Self-Publishers & Craftspeople

For some of you this is your first business tax season; others have run their business this way for years. Most of you work alone, or maybe your spouse helps with the paperwork. And, there never seem to be enough hours in the day to get everything done.

As April 15th gets close most small business owners get stressed out, and the sole-proprietor is forced to stop working in order to deal with the confusing pile of receipts and paperwork that sits between you and that quickly approaching tax deadline.

This organizer will show you how to whip that pile of paperwork into shape quickly so that you can satisfy the IRS and get right back to work. It teaches you a simple once-a-year method for organizing small business income and expense records and explains exactly what the IRS expects of a self-employed business person.

The situations and examples used in this book include a variety of barber and beauty shop business styles in an attempt to provide information that could be applied to all types of self-employment situations.

Plus, the recordkeeping system designed for this book makes getting your business records organized at tax time quick and easy.

If you are selling hair care or beauty products to your clientele you'll also find lots of inventory examples that will help you to understand how the IRS expects you to account for and expense those inventory costs.

And, for the salon owner, this book also includes lots of situational examples to help you get a clear understanding of exactly what the IRS expects, so that you can turn in audit-proof tax returns year after year.

Step by step this Annual Tax Mess Organizer will walk you through the tax-time sorting process of income, expenses and other needed information, helping you to get everything organized and ready for your tax preparer.

The independent business owner who have always done their own personal tax return will even find a chapter on how to fill out a Schedule C small business federal tax form.

It walks you through the form line by line, explaining where to post all of the information you've gathered, helping you with supporting tax forms, and showing you where to post the final figures onto your 1040 personal tax return.

If you've deposited all of your business income into just one bank account, and kept all of your expense receipts together in one place, this organizer will have you ready for your tax preparer in less than 3 hours. Even if your records are a total mess you should be done in 4-5 hours, once you've located all of the necessary paperwork and receipts.

You'll also find a chapter on Developing an Audit-Proof Mindset which explains how easy it is to win a tax audit, and teaches you a simple method for keeping your business returns audit proof.

What You Need

No computer is required for this system, and all of the forms you'll need for organizing and recording your annual tax information have been included as well. This system will work for anyone; basic math is the only skill you need to use this Annual Tax Mess Organizer to get your business records ready at tax time.

You will also need the following:

25 large envelopes

Adding machine

Empty table or desktop

The envelopes can be 6x9 if you don't have a lot of receipts; use larger envelopes if your business generates a bigger pile of paperwork. If you don't have large envelopes on hand, and your pile of paperwork is small, you can substitute 25 #10 business letter-sized envelopes.

If you purchase an adding machine with a paper tape you'll make fewer mistakes. Running a paper tape twice is a terrific way to check your math; when the numbers don't match you've entered something wrong. Add them again until you get two paper tapes with matching totals.

The organization process used with this Annual Tax Mess Organizer is very simple, and only requires you to deal with your income and expense paperwork once a year. The rest of the time all you need to do is practice good habits when it comes to making bank deposits and purchases for your business. And, all of that is explained in this book.

To make all of your future tax seasons simple we now offer a book that contains all of the simple organizer forms found in this book, and it's a three-year organizer. With the **Annual Tax Mess Organizer 3-Year Form Book** you'll have all of the income, expense, inventory and annual tax forms you need for the next three years.

Now let's get down to business!

INCOME AND EXPENSE TRACKING MADE EASY

Income Tracking the Simple Way

To survive an IRS audit you need to maintain a separate checking account for your business. Otherwise, the IRS can question every single deposit and expense co-mingled with your personal funds, and your tax bill may be higher than necessary.

Tracking business income is a snap once you learn to follow Tax Pro Rule #1.

Tax Pro Rule #1

**Absolutely all business income,
including all cash & tips,
must be deposited into a separate checking account
used only for business funds.**

Many banks offer free checking, and it makes no difference to the IRS whether this account is in your personal or business name. So, if you don't already have one, open a business account today and follow Tax Pro Rule #1.

Expense Tracking the Simple Way

Tracking business expenses is just as easy. All you need to do is always follow Tax Pro Rule #2.

Tax Pro Rule #2

**Every penny spent or charged for your business
needs a paper trail. If a receipt
is not provided you can make your own.**

When you use your debit card or write a check you leave a paper trail, but following that trail a year later can be confusing. It's a lot easier to work from actual receipts.

Getting a receipt for every purchase is the best method, but you can make your own when a receipt is not available. If you create your own receipt you will need to include the date, how much money you spent, what you purchased and who got the money. Carry a small spiral notepad in your car for little purchases; you can sort and total them at tax time. Keep an envelope in the car too, for stashing loose receipts.

Follow those first two Tax Pro Rules all year long and you'll cut your tax preparation time in half next year.

TRACKING INCOME FOR THE IRS

If you already have a separate checking account, and you deposited all of your business income into that account, all you need to track your income are your 12 bank statements for the tax year.

At the end of this chapter you'll find a 2-page form titled *Business Income - End of Year Report*. It includes space to write the total monthly deposit figure from each bank statement, as well as other business income. Total those together and you will know your total business income as deposited for the tax year, which you will need in order to prepare your annual tax return.

Get one of your large envelopes and write BUSINESS INCOME across the top. Write that total deposit amount for the tax year on the front of this envelope and put all of those bank statements inside. Business bank statements should always be stored right along with your other business tax receipts and records. You will also want to add your checkbook register to this envelope later.

If you do any barter (trading your goods or business services with another for goods or services) that too must be reported as income according to IRS rules. Tax Pro Rule #3 is about barter income.

Tax Pro Rule #3

**Every business barter exchange requires
a paper trail assigning value to your time,
or the product you traded
for another's time or product.**

You are expected to count as business income the value of every single barter exchange that you make in business. The value of a barter exchange is what you would have charged if that person had paid you in cash. If you trade goods or inventory during a barter exchange those costs will be deducted along with other expenses; for now we're only concerned with your barter income.

You can itemize your barter exchanges on the second page of the *Business Income - End of Year Report* located at the end of this chapter. You will also need to post the total to the front of the Business Income envelope and label it Barter Income.

If you collect rent from other people or businesses in exchange for part of your business workspace you will need to list that income separately on both your *Business Income - End of Year Report* as well as on the front of your Business Income envelope. Space rent received in a business where you also work is always posted to your Small Business Schedule C Tax Form, and not to the IRS rental property form.

Looking for Income

If you weren't very well organized last year you're not totally out of luck; it will just take you a little longer to figure out how much money you made in your business. Most income can be found by answering two simple questions.

Income Question #1: Where did you deposit the checks?

The first place to look would be in your personal bank account. Grab the checkbook register and highlight every deposit that you made with business income. Total up all of those business deposits and enter that number on the front of your Business Income envelope as well as the *Business Income - End of Year Report*. Be sure to note which bank account those business funds were deposited into if you are using more than one bank account.

You will need to save those personal checkbook registers along with your other business receipts in case of a tax audit. If you have deposited business income into more than one personal bank account repeat the above procedure on each account.

Because you have co-mingled funds the burden of proof will be on you, if an audit is called for by the IRS. If an audit happens you could be required to prove to the IRS that every other deposit made into your personal bank accounts were not business income as well.

Paychecks will be easy, but any cash gifts or other unsubstantiated deposits will cause problems, and could be taxed as business income. The bottom line in an audit is, if you can't prove otherwise the auditor can count co-mingled deposits as business income.

This is one of the biggest reasons why you need to open a business checking account, to keep the IRS out of your personal banking business.

Income Question #2: What did you do with the cash?

Cash income can be tricky.

Business income is taxed whether you receive it as a check, cash, barter, or in any other form. The government wants their share, and if the IRS comes looking and you have no records you could end up paying taxes you don't actually owe.

For most independent business people writing all cash income on a calendar every single time they are paid in cash is enough proof for the IRS. Consistency in reporting is the key for calendar-style reporting. Someone who is running a retail store would need a register-style cash reporting system; the calendar method is only for people who receive occasional cash or regular tip income.

Barbers, hair stylists and sometimes even the salon owner will get tips from their customers; some could be generous but others might be cheap. Just remember, if you are working in an industry where it is normal to receive tips the IRS will expect to see tips reported on your tax return.

If you don't actually track your tip income, and you're called for an audit, unless you can prove differently you'll be taxed based on the standard tip rate for your industry. The cash calendar is perfect for tracking and proving actual tip income as long as you make an entry on this calendar every day that you work, even if that amount is zero.

You also need to deposit ALL of your cash income into your business bank account. You can do this daily, weekly or as needed, but if you don't make those deposits you'll end up in tax trouble during an audit.

When you use a calendar for tracking your cash income it is important to record every penny of cash income on that calendar, or this calendar can be disqualified. And when that happens, the IRS rules state that when you do not account for all cash income in a consistent manner they get to decide how much cash income you made, based on industry standards.

If you get audited and you did not keep proper records you're sunk. All you can do is make a plan to keep better records in the future, do your best to come up with the right amount this year, and cross your fingers that you're not audited.

Post the total of all of the cash income that you find onto the front of your Business Income envelope as well as to the *Business Income - End of Year Report* located at the end of this chapter.

Put all of your paperwork, including any cash calendars, into the Business Income envelope as well.

Computing Your Gross Business Income

All you need to do now is add up all of your bank deposits, barter values, space rent and cash income that you have posted onto your *Business Income -End of Year Report*.

This total is what the IRS refers to as your Gross Business Income. It is not your taxable business income; there's a lot more work to be done before you'll know what amount will be taxed, if any.

Write your Total Gross Income on your *Business Income - End of Year Report*. You will also need to write this total on the front of your Business Income envelope. You are finished with the report for now. You will come back to this report later for that Total Gross Income figure.

Set the Business Income envelope aside too; you won't need it again. You'll learn what to do with these envelopes and all about proper tax record storage in the chapter on developing an audit-proof mindset.

BUSINESS INCOME - END OF YEAR REPORT

TAX YEAR _____

Bank Account #1

Jan. $ _____

Feb. $ _____

March $ _____

April $ _____

May $ _____

June $ _____

July $ _____

Aug. $ _____

Sept. $ _____

Oct. $ _____

Nov. $ _____

Dec. $ _____

Total $ _____

Bank Account #2

Jan. $ _____

Feb. $ _____

March $ _____

April $ _____

May $ _____

June $ _____

July $ _____

Aug. $ _____

Sept. $ _____

Oct. $ _____

Nov. $ _____

Dec. $ _____

Total $ _____

DO NOT include any deposits that were not business income. This would include any funds deposited that you borrowed, as well as any personal funds that you deposited to cover your business bills. These are not income; these deposits would be considered loans. List any loans that need to be subtracted from the bank deposit totals here:

Cash Income (not deposited in bank) - $_____

Barter Income - List by job name and include the total value for each barter income exchange:

Space Rent Income - List by payer name and include the total year's rent received from each person. (If all rent was included in bank deposits **DO NOT** add this amount to the total income because it is already included in your bank deposit totals.)

Total Gross Income - Add all income deposited into each bank account together with the total value of all barter income and list that total below. **DO NOT** include amounts listed under space rent or loans if those payments were deposited into your business bank account.

1) Total of all bank accounts minus any loans $_____

2) Total of all cash income not deposited & barter values $_____

3) All space rent not included in the bank deposit $_____

     TOTAL GROSS INCOME FOR THE YEAR $_____

TRACKING EXPENSES FOR THE IRS

How fast you get done with this step depends on whether or not you have kept your receipts organized throughout the year. When it's easy for you to get your hands on your business expense receipts this task doesn't take long at all.

If all you did was shove your receipts into an envelope, drawer or box you're actually in luck. All you need to do now is sort those receipts, and this book teaches you how to do that quickly.

For the totally unorganized business owner now is the time when you're forced to search high and low for any receipt or recollection of money that you spent on your business. Here are some good places to look.

Start with your checkbook register, credit card records, debit statements and bank accounts; highlight all business expenses. Dig thru your car, coat pockets, briefcase or purse, and anywhere else you normally shove papers to see if any receipts have been left there, as well as your personal receipt files.

If you have clients, and purchase goods to complete work for them, you may find expense receipts mixed in with your client records. Look around your place of business to jog your memory for equipment purchased during the tax year, and in general do everything you can to locate receipts and reconstruct expense records.

Business expenses are generally 100% deductible from your gross business income. But, you must know what you spent in order to take advantage of that deduction. Guessing is not allowed; without a paper trail you will fail an IRS audit.

If you want to pay less in taxes take the time to track down every legitimate expense. The tax savings could easily be several hundred dollars.

Organizing Expense Receipts

Sorting expense receipts is simple once you learn Annual Tax Mess Organizer's business expense alphabet. This book teaches you a simple ABC sorting procedure that is quick and easy.

Tax Pro Rule #4

**Sorting expense receipts
is as easy as ABC when you use
the business expense alphabet.**

To help you organize your expense receipts quickly you're going to label the rest of those large envelopes and use them as guides when you sort your expense receipts.

All totals will be written onto the front of those envelopes, and eventually all of the matching receipts will be tucked inside.

Creating Your Expense Envelopes

Across the top of each envelope write one of the alphabetical titles from the list below. Use a dark pen so you can see it quickly, and keep it near the top of the envelope so that it won't get covered by papers when you sort your receipts.

Each envelope represents a deductible expense classification as defined by the IRS.

A   Advertising & Promotional Expenses

B   Bank, Visa & Other Business Interest Paid

C   Cleaning Materials & Business Supplies

D   Donations to Nonprofit Organizations

E   Educational Seminars & Classes

F   Fix-it & Repair Expenses

G   Gifts

H   Home Office Expenses

I   Insurance

J   Job Required Licenses & Dues

L   Legal & Professional Fees

M Meals & Entertainment

N   Newspapers, Magazines & Subscriptions

O   Office Supplies

P   People Who Take a Share

Q   Equipment Purchased

R   Rent Paid

S   Shipping & Postage

T   Travel

U   Utilities

V   Vehicle (Car/Truck) Expenses

W Wages & Contract Labor Expenses

X   Taxes & Business Licenses

Z   Inventory

Now that you have all of your expense envelopes labeled read the following information explaining which expenses belong in each category. When you're finished you'll be ready to sort your expense receipts.

What is Deductible?

To be considered a business you must be profit motivated. Otherwise you can be classified as a hobbyist by the IRS.

Hobby income is not taxed the same way as business income because the hobbyist's intent is not considered to be profit motivated. Because of this, the IRS classifies hobby income as miscellaneous income and not business income. Hobby expenses are limited to the posted hobby income, but when you are in business your losses are generally not limited.

The small business owner who repeatedly posts a business loss could be asked to prove that he or she is intent on building a business and actively seeking income. This is easy to prove when you have a written business plan.

IRS rules allow a business owner to deduct all ordinary and necessary expenses that are incurred during the production of, or attempt to produce, any legitimate income. Business profit or loss is calculated using the IRS Schedule C tax form; that figure is then posted directly onto your 1040 personal tax return.

The small business owner can also deduct all of the expenses involved in operating a home office, business mileage or expenses and depreciation on vehicles, and interest on business-only debts, including credit cards and home equity mortgages.

If you purchase self-employed health insurance or make IRA or other retirement deposits, these costs will be posted to your personal 1040 tax return and not your Schedule C business return.

Self-employment taxes, which fund your Social Security and Medicare accounts, when owed on business income are also posted to your 1040 tax return.

Be sure to take all of the figures for your health insurance costs and retirement fund contributions with you when you visit your tax professional. These too will lower your income tax bill.

If you are preparing your own tax return you'll need to add those expenses to your 1040 and calculate your self-employment tax as well. In this book's chapter on preparing your own small business tax return you'll learn how to calculate self-employment taxes and exactly where all of those other business deductions are posted.

The more a business owner knows about what they can deduct, the quicker the sorting process will go, and the more items you will deduct with confidence. Remember, for every legitimate expense you subtract you will decrease your taxable income and keep more money in your own pocket. And that makes it a very worthwhile activity.

Read the following ABC expense category descriptions before you begin sorting your expense receipts.

A - Advertising & Promotional Expenses

This category includes all business cards, print and online phone book ads, newspaper & magazine ads, flyer inserts, school or sport sponsorships, coupon books, refrigerator magnets and all other money spent to promote or advertise your business.

If you spent money or traded goods (or an employee's services) to get your business name or product out in front of the public, it's deductible. For the salon owner this would include paying an employee to give free haircuts or even paid haircuts at a festival or other public event.

For a barber or hair stylist promotional expenses would include all hair care or other products purchased for use on your clients during special events where you promote your business.

This would include any product used while giving free haircuts at a local non-profit shelter, custom-printed hair tiebacks that help to advertise your salon, and all fees paid to enter a competition that would promote your salon as well as the expenses involved in getting to that event and setting up a display.

For barber and beauty shop owners this category also includes all holiday decorations, holiday treats for the reception area, salon publicity, and fees paid to marketing consultants hired to promote the shop.

A salon owner would also claim all money spent to get into an event or show where the stylists could be promoted. Everything you do to promote your salon is considered an advertising or promotional expense, and this includes social networking. So, if you pay someone to tweet about your services, post photos on Pinterest to showcase your work, or set up your business Facebook profile, it's deducted here.

B - Bank, Visa & Other Business Interest Paid

Monthly checking account fees, bank business account overdraft penalties, business credit card finance charges, annual credit card fees and business debt interest all get deducted in this category.

Check all of your bank, credit card and loan statements for these charges; this is a deduction that is often overlooked and under reported. If you take out a home equity loan to finance your business all of the costs involved in getting that loan, as well as all interest charged on that loan, becomes a business deduction.

C - Cleaning Materials & Business Supplies

This category includes all of your work space cleaning supplies, organizing bins, light bulbs, operating supplies, and even coffee for your clients. It also includes of the supplies necessary to produce income in your particular profession. This will vary depending upon your industry.

Business supplies normally include all items you need to perform your work, with the exception of office supplies, overhead (utilities and rent), and business equipment that you have not deducted elsewhere. Those expenses are reported in other categories.

A cosmetologist would include towels, shampoo, color and perm supplies;; a barber includes shaving supplies, hot towels and hair care products.

Beauty shop and salon workers should include all expenses necessary to prepare for and perform client treatments that are not deducted elsewhere. If you bought an item to use in your work, it is a deductible expense.

Any tool you buy that cost less than $75 belongs in this category; more expensive tools are considered equipment by the IRS and reported in another category.

A salon owner will have lots of non-styling business supplies as well.

This might include appointment books, time cards for employees, scheduling calendars, software to manage appointments or bookkeeping, and other managerial supplies.

Whether you're a barber, cosmetologist or salon owner, it makes no difference; you're all looking for items purchased to enable you to perform your job, those things you bought with the specific purpose of preparing to perform your job, and everything you bought to clean up after doing your job.

All of those items are deductible as cleaning materials and business supplies, when you work in the hair care industry.

D - Donations to Nonprofit Organizations

All small business donations are taken on the owner's personal tax return; they do not get posted to your Schedule C business return.

Donations of goods or artwork with a value of $5,000 or more must always include a qualified appraisal for each item donated. You only need an appraisal summary, unless the value exceeds $20,000, then you will need the complete appraisal.

Some donations can be considered as an advertising expense. This is the case when you make a donation for the express purpose of promoting your business. When this happens, this expense should be deducted at tax time as advertising.

Your personal labor or time is never deductible as a donation. However, if you pay someone and donate their labor that expense is tax deductible. Products donated are deducted at cost as removed from inventory, and not their full retail price.

E - Educational Seminars & Classes

Seminars and classes that will help make you better at what you do to produce income, as well as general business classes, are all deductible.

Remember to record all mileage or travel expenses if you have them; those will be reported along with other mileage and travel expenses. If you only have one receipt for all of those expenses simply make copies for other expense categories and highlight the deductions that should be taken on each category copy.

A beauty shop or salon owner would include all operating, promotional and educational seminars attended. A barber or stylist includes any classes taken to retain his or her license or to improve their skills, including technique and business classes.

If a hair stylist takes hair color classes or enrolls in a professional seminar offered by a hair care company, those costs belong here. All professional studies, seminars and business classes, whether online or attended in person, are educational business expenses.

F - Fix-it & Repair Expenses

Equipment repairs, the cost involved in fixing a broken desk drawer, and all of your other repair or fix-it expenses belong in this category. If you pay a computer expert to solve a computer problem, that's a fix-it expense. When someone comes out to repair the window air conditioner in your shop, that expense is deducted here as well.

A salon owner would deduct salon repairs. A barber who ordered replacement parts for his clippers would include the cost of those parts here, even though he may have installed them himself.

A hair stylist who paid someone to sharpen her scissors or fix the lift on her chair would put that receipt here.

Every self-employed and independent worker has equipment that could break; any repair or parts expense necessary to fix that equipment is deducted in this category.

G - Gifts

Each year you can deduct up to $25 per client or vendor, when you give gifts to that client or vendor. You must make a note on the back of the receipt for the item given, and include the receiver's name.

Cookies and candy that you put out for all of your customers who visit are not gifts; those are business supplies and belong in category C.

Meals you take part in do not count as gifts either, they are deducted as meals. If instead you give your client a restaurant gift card, that would be considered a gift. Items taken from your own inventory are not deducted as gifts either, those are deducted from inventory on a cost per item basis. This is explained in the section on tracking inventory.

H - Home Office Expenses

If you use one room or more in your home exclusively for business, you may be able to deduct a portion of your home operating expenses. This includes your rent or the interest and property taxes paid on your home, plus household insurance, all shared utilities, lawn maintenance and cleaning. Any item used 100% by the business can be 100% expensed.

How much you get to deduct for shared expenses is based on the size of your home versus the space devoted exclusively to the business. Annual totals for each home office expense should be written on the front of the Home Office Expense envelope after you sort your receipts; the IRS requires that all home office expenses be listed separately.

If you own your own home you need to discuss the disadvantages of depreciating your home office with a tax professional before taking this portion of the home office deduction. Don't overlook this, because taking your home office depreciation will affect the taxes due when you sell your home since you will not be able to exclude that portion of your personal residence profit from income taxes.

You do not have to depreciate your home in order to take the other home office deductions.

I - Insurance

All business and liability insurance costs are expensed here. Health insurance is not. If you have self-employed health insurance costs they will be reported on the front of your 1040 personal return, not on your business tax return.

J - Job Required Licenses & Dues

Business and license fees, union dues, and membership dues paid to any professional or business networking organization are all included in category J. If you need a city business license for your business, that expense goes here; a barber or hair stylist license also belongs in this category.

L - Legal & Professional Fees

All bookkeeping, payroll service expenses and legal fees incurred by your business are deductible at tax time. That would include any entrepreneur or small business owner who pays an attorney to look over a contract or prepare legal papers; it does not include personal legal expenses.

Hiring a bookkeeping service to handle your accounting paperwork or payroll is also included in this category.

Payment for tax preparation should be included here too, but only the portion that applies to your business tax return.

M - Meals & Entertainment

If you take clients or business associates out to lunch, dinner or for entertainment in order to improve your business relationship it could be deductible at tax time. But, you must always write the client or associate's name on the back of your receipt, as well as a short description of what business you discussed if you want to win a tax audit. Business meals are only 50% deductible.

Meals eaten during overnight travel will need to be totaled separately.

The IRS per diem rates are often a better way for a small business owner to expense their travel meals using the current IRS per diem figures; the per diem method requires less work but can only be applied to overnight travel meals. It is never used for regular business meals.

Entertainment expenses included in this category are those that you attended along with your client. This could be anything from a baseball game or sporting event to a play or opera, as long as you take that client or vendor for the purpose of improving your business relationship. Again, it is important to note the client's name and business discussed on the receipt.

If you do not attend, but merely give tickets to a vendor or client, those tickets would be categorized as either a gift or promotional expense, and those receipts would then be sorted to category G if a gift or category A if promotion. Always consider the $25 limitation before classifying any entertainment as a gift.

Example #1: *Gerald enjoys working with bridal parties. He buys a block of tickets to the annual bridal show, and gives them to people who are engaged and planning their wedding. Gerald does this because he wants them to hire him to do hair for the entire wedding party. He even has a Bridal Party Special.*

Gerald is trying to get work, and that makes those tickets a promotional expense, not an entertainment expense.

Example #2: *Judy is a hair stylist who agreed to work on a celebrity wedding 300 miles away from home. She kept her apartment while she was gone, and stayed in a hotel so that she could be on hand to give massages to family and bridal party members who came to town for the 10-day event.*

All travel and motel expenses will end up in the Travel envelope, but the meal receipts for those 10 nights that Judy spent at the wedding location need to be lumped together in the meal category, with a notation about the length of time spent away from home on this out of town job.

When Judy's taxes were prepared, the standard meal allowance rate for overnight trips was $46 a day in most U.S. cities. Rather than add up all of the fast food, restaurant and drive-thru coffee stand receipts Judy had, plus her notes about late-night stops at convenience stores for food and snacks she remembered, but had no receipts for, her accountant simply multiplied $46 times 10 days. Then he took half of that $460 standard meal allowance for a deduction of $230.

N - Newspapers, Magazines & Subscriptions

Magazines, newspapers and newsletters that you purchase to increase your business knowledge get deducted in this category. They do not have to be printed; online subscriptions count as well.

This includes every magazine you read to stay current on your specific industry, as well as all hair care magazines, hair styling technique subscriptions, salon magazines, and business magazine subscriptions.

O - Office Supplies

Office supplies are different from business supplies. Business supplies are specific to your trade or industry; office supplies are used by all small businesses. Dictionaries and office reference books, printer paper, photocopies, adding machine tape, computer supplies, paper clips, staples, pens, notepads, appointment books, and other desk or office supplies belong here. The cost of this organizer can be included in this category since it tames the paperwork.

If you pay another business to send your faxes, that too is an office supply expense.

P - People Who Take a Share

You only use this category if your payments are processed by an agent who takes a cut of the total before issuing your payment, or if you are required to pay a fee to someone who sells your services or product. This would be rare in your profession as a hair stylist or barber.

If you are working in a spa, shop or salon that collects all of your client payments and then pays you a percentage of what you earn, you could enter those commissions here. But don't, because that commission was never actually paid to you in the first place, it was subtracted before the check was issued.

Never enter a commission in this category that was not first recorded and deposited as income. When you deposit a check where the commission has already been deducted, your bank account only reflects the income you deposited, and not the percentage withheld by someone who takes a share.

Those commissions could show up in the total that was put on the 1099 you received, but because you are working directly from your income deposits they won't show up in your income.

If you are sent a commission statement at the end of the year, keep it with all of your other income paperwork in case of an audit. If the commission was entered as income received you will need to ask that person to issue a new 1099 so that the IRS will not expect you to pay taxes on money that was never received. It's wise to remember that not everyone who issues 1099's knows how to fill them out properly.

Q - Equipment Purchased

Any furniture or equipment that you buy for your business, including desks, file cabinets, computers, cameras, calculators, printers, desk lamps, a waiting area couch, office artwork, display equipment, etc. must be expensed over its expected life according to IRS rules.

Tax Pro Rule #5

**Any equipment purchased,
with an expected life of two or more years
must be depreciated or expensed
as a Section 179 deduction.**

The general rule is, if it will be used for two or more years and costs more than $75 it will need to go into this category for a tax return depreciation deduction. In most cases you can still deduct the entire expense all at once using a technique the IRS calls the Section 179 deduction.

Your tax professional will need to know the date of purchase and the cost of each tool or piece of equipment you buy before preparing your business tax return. Itemize all big purchases on the outside of your Equipment envelope when you sort, making sure to include all of the information required.

R - Rent Paid

If you are buying your shop building you will include all interest paid on the business mortgage in this category. Also post this information on the front of the "R" envelope.

If you pay rent for chair space, rent tools or equipment, pay for storage space or have other rent expenses include all of those costs in this category.

Home office expenses do not belong in this category; they go in the "H" envelope.

S - Shipping & Postage

Stamps purchased to send out business mail, as well as any UPS, FedEx or other shipping or transport fees paid to send out products or business materials belong in the "S" envelope. Many independent business people use personal stamps to send out business bills. Buy your own business stamps and take the deduction. If you pay shipping to receive an item purchased for inventory that expense will be included with your other inventory expenses.

If you receive payments for shipping along with orders and you deposit the entire payment received all of your shipping payments will be reflected as business income. By deducting all of your shipping expenses incurred in sending the product to your customer you remove those shipping payments from income.

T - Travel

All business trips and seminar travel expenses, including airfare, tips, taxi or bus, parking, entry fees and hotel expenses are deductible travel expenses.

Taking your spouse along for pleasure does not make his or her portion of the trip deductible; only your portion will be tax deductible. If a trip includes both business and pleasure days only a portion of those travel expenses can be deducted.

Overnight business trip meals are also deductible, but those need to be listed as a separate total for proper income tax reporting.

If you are away for business overnight write the total number of nights you spent out of town on the front of your Travel envelope, as well as the total amount that you spent for your overnight travel meals.

Put the actual travel meal receipts with your "M" envelope; clip them together and tag them overnight business meal receipts, keeping them separate from regular meal receipts.

If you travel often for business, when your taxes are prepared ask your tax preparer if the IRS per diem rate established for business meal deductions would be a better way for you to expense those overnight meals. It often is!

U - Utilities

If you rent a shop or office space and pay utilities, they are deducted here. This includes the shop or business electricity, water, internet fees, heat, garbage, telephone, and cable tv or music subscription fees that are used at the office.

All business long distance telephone charges, as well as the cost of a 2nd telephone line at home or a cell phone used exclusively for business can be deducted here. The cost of your primary home telephone is not deductible, even if you use it for business.

Home office utilities do not belong in this envelope; they belong in the "H" envelope along with other home office expenses.

V - Vehicle (Car & Truck) Expenses

If you keep good mileage records you'll pay a lot less tax. That's because for every 100 miles you drive for your business you get to subtract more than $50 as an expense.

Tax Pro Rule #6

**Unless you have a vehicle used only for business
keep a notebook in the car
and write down every business mile.**

Business miles include every single trip you make to pick up business or office supplies, drop off business mail, transport a client, or attend professional classes or seminars. Those little trips to drop bills at the post office or run to the office supply store for paper add up quickly and, with the cost of gas you don't want to miss a single mile. This deduction can be huge if you spend lots of time in your car.

If you kept a mileage log whenever you ran your business errands simply add up all of the miles in that mileage log and post the total as deductible business miles. Your total vehicle miles can be approximated if you have your actual business miles written down.

Write your total miles driven for the business on the front of the "V" envelope.

If you are able to devote one vehicle exclusively to your business all you will need are the odometer numbers at the beginning of year (BOY) and the end of year (EOY). If you took the mileage deduction last year that EOY mileage figure on last year's tax return will become your BOY figure for this year.

If this is your first year in business and you didn't write the opening mileage down at the start of your business year check repair or oil change receipts, they may show your mileage, and you can figure it out from there.

If more than half of all of the miles put on a vehicle are business-related miles you should also track your actual vehicle expenses to see if this is a better deduction. To take the actual vehicle expenses, or depreciate your vehicle, you will need to itemize all of your vehicle's expenses on the front of the "V" envelope and save all your receipts. Those actual vehicle expenses might include car payments, repair costs, tires or parts purchased, auto insurance, vehicle registration fees, gas, oil, and any other costs involved in operating your car or truck.

If you use more than one vehicle in your business keep track of the miles driven in each vehicle. Note each vehicle's miles separately on the front of this expense envelope as well as your tax return.

W - Wages & Contract Labor Expenses

If you have employees find a quality bookkeeping service; most will handle all of the regulatory paperwork for a small fee. Payroll requires regular deposits of taxes withheld as well as tax deposits for the matching sums owed by the employer. Most small business owners don't have the time to add payroll to their To Do List. There are lots of qualified bookkeeping companies who offer this service.

At the end of the calendar year they can furnish payroll reports showing where all of the payroll money went that did not go directly to the employee. This report should include all federal, FICA, Medicare, workman comp, state and other taxes paid as well as payroll totals for each employee. You will need these numbers when your income tax return is prepared; put all payroll reports in the "W" envelope after writing all of those totals on the front.

When you hire independent contractors who are not incorporated the IRS requires you to complete a 1099M tax form reporting all money paid to each individual when you pay them $600 or more during any tax year. These forms can be purchased from any office supply store. You must mail a copy to those individuals by January 31st. A copy must also be sent to the IRS.

If you get caught avoiding payroll taxes by claiming that an employee is an independent contractor the IRS can fine you heavily and make you pay all unpaid taxes, even those normally paid by the employee.

Someone who works exclusively for you, on your time schedule, doing a job exactly the way you instruct, using your tools or office space, is probably not an independent contractor. You may have an employee, even if that person only works a few hours a week, and that means you are required to classify them as an employee and follow all laws regarding employees and payroll.

If you are confused about the difference between an independent contractor and an employee discuss this with a tax professional. An error in classification today could be expensive later. The IRS provides free help at www.IRS.gov too.

X - Taxes & Business Licenses

The letter T was already used and since taxes are by law required to be eXact the letter "X" was chosen to represent taxes. This category is where you enter all of your state sales taxes, city taxes and any other taxes that you paid for your business.

Don't forget to include your federal and/or state income tax quarterly payments. If you pay property taxes on your business building, they too belong here.

Any license that is required by the state, county or city in order for you to operate your business, or practice your profession also gets sorted into this category. Your car or truck license does not belong here. If you are expensing your vehicle that license receipt would go with your other vehicle expenses for deducting.

Z - Inventory

The IRS considers any item you make or purchase for resale to be inventory. Items purchased for a particular customer as well as items you buy to complete a job are not considered to be inventory.

Tax Pro Rule #7

**All items purchased or created for resale
are considered to be inventory by the IRS.
Inventory expenses can only be deducted
as that inventory is sold.**

Inventory expenses are deducted on a cost per item basis, and not deducted completely until every item is either sold or removed from inventory. As you sort through your receipts pull every receipt that has anything to do with the purchase or creation of inventory, including shipping charges, and put them into this category.

Someone who sells hair or skin care products would have inventory; all unsold items remaining in stock at the end of the tax year is considered to be your end of year inventory.

If you do not buy items for resale you will not have inventory. If you sell everything the same year that you purchase it there is also no inventory. But, if you make an item in bulk and sell it individually you will have inventory if <u>any</u> of your stock remains on your shelves on the last work day of the year.

A salon owner, barber or hair stylist who makes or stocks beauty supplies to sell to her clients would have inventory. An barber or hairstylist rarely has inventory, unless they purchase hair care or other products for resale, in which case those items would be considered inventory.

If you are devoting part of your business space to regular inventory production you will need to include a portion of your overhead along with inventory production expenses. The wages of an employee who assembled that inventory would also be included with your inventory production expenses. If you have either of these inventory expenses see a tax professional for help with your inventory calculations.

At the end of each tax year you are required to count all remaining inventory, both on your shelves and out for sale on consignment. Your end-of-year (EOY) inventory value and inventory count for this tax year will become the beginning-of-year (BOY) inventory count and inventory value on next year's tax return.

Sorting Your Expense Receipts

Once you understand those ABC categories and have your expense envelopes labeled lay those expense envelopes out on an empty table or desk. Eliminate any envelopes that you know you won't use. For example, you may not have inventory, home office deductions, people who take a share or meal expenses. That would take four envelopes off the table.

Space the remaining envelopes far enough apart to avoid mixing paperwork when you sort. You are now ready to begin sorting your receipts.

Go through all of your receipts one-by-one and decide where each receipt belongs; lay each receipt on top of the matching expense envelope. You may discover that some receipts could be classified in more than one way; unless this book tells you otherwise just choose the category that you think fits best.

To make the sort go quicker put anything you cannot immediately classify into a "second run" pile. After sorting all of your easy receipts go back to that stack and try again. If there are any receipts that you can't figure out simply clip them together -- they can be dealt with individually when your taxes are prepared.

If you run an inventory remember to sort all of the expense receipts involved in receiving and producing that inventory onto the "Z" envelope, even though it may also qualify for another category.

Most of your small business expense receipts will easily fall into one of those 24 expense categories.

Posting Business Deductions

In the next chapter you will post all of your expense envelope totals onto an Annual Tax Report. You will want to start by adding up all of the receipts in each category and writing that total onto the front of each envelope.

Once you have written the total on any expense envelope tuck the receipts inside. You will not need to open that envelope again unless you find an additional receipt since everything you need is now listed on the front.

If you discover additional receipts simply scratch out the old total and write the new one on the envelope before putting those receipts inside. You will need to change that total anywhere else you have written it as well.

When you're all done with your taxes you will store all of your expense envelopes in a bag or box marked Tax Receipts. Rules for keeping tax receipts as well as storage tips are addressed in the Developing an Audit-Proof Mindset chapter of this book.

Tracking Inventory

Any time you add new or additional inventory a "per item" cost must be calculated for that item. You calculate your per item cost by dividing the total amount spent to add that product to your inventory by the number of pieces that were added.

You are required by IRS rules to count all of your inventory at the close of each tax year and to produce inventory records if requested during a tax audit.

Here are a few real-life examples of how inventory costs are calculated.

Example #1: John stocks a special line of hair gel in his barber shop. He got free shipping with his first 75 jar order; the invoice total was $168.75, or $2.25 per item. In August John placed a second 75 jar order, and with shipping his bill came to $172.50. Those jars had a value of $2.30 each.

John sold 120 jars of gel; there were 30 jars remaining on the shelf at the end of the tax year. He deducts the entire cost paid for the first 75 jar order; that was the $168.75 invoice.

The remaining 45 jars are expensed at $2.30 each, the cost per item based on the second shipment received. Those 45 jars receive a $103.50 deduction.

Our barber takes this $272.25 deduction this year, and when the remaining jars are sold next year he deducts the final $69.00. It sounds confusing, but because John tracks the cost and quantity of each shipment as it arrives, all he does is total a few columns at the end of the year.

Example #2: Laura sells jewelry in her beauty shop. She buys a lot of cheaper pieces from an importer, but also sells nicer hand-beaded earrings made by a friend. All of her friend's earrings sell for $30 a pair. Laura does not pay her friend until her earrings are sold. Every time she sells a pair of earrings she tucks $15 into an envelope for her friend and $15 into her own cash box. Her friend's earrings are not inventory for Laura; they are being sold on consignment and do not belong to Laura, they still belong to her friend.

The imported pieces however are inventory because Laura buys them for resale. If all pieces in a shipment are identical Laura can simply divide the number of pieces received into the total cost to get her cost per item. If the shipment contains non-conforming items the calculation will be a little more time consuming. Each item, along with a portion of all shipping costs, must be tracked and expensed separately. All of the imported pieces remaining in Laura's shop at the end of the year will not be expensed until sold.

Example #3: Mandy bottles and sells an herbal shampoo she makes herself. She sold it in her shop, and online as well. She got a late start her first year, putting her shampoo up for sale in December and only sold 150 bottles that first year, plus she gave another 50 bottles away as gifts to long-time clients. But the shampoo was a hit and sold out before the end of the following tax year.

To make 1200 bottles of shampoo Mandy bought $1500 worth of ingredients and paid $1200 for bottles and lids. She mixed and bottled the shampoo herself, at home in her kitchen. To get her cost per bottle of shampoo, Mandy adds the cost of the ingredients and bottles together ($2700) and divides this by the 1200 bottles she was able to package. Her cost per item is $2.25 each.

The first year, even though she spent $2700 she can only write off the cost of the 200 bottles of shampoo removed from inventory. Her deduction is $450. Because Mandy sells the other 1000 bottles the following tax year she can deduct the remaining $2250 on her next tax return.

Creating a New Inventory Report

To track new inventory you will need to create a New Inventory Report. On the next three pages you will find a blank New Inventory Report. Instructions follow.

NEW INVENTORY REPORT
(All new items added to inventory during tax year)

(1) Product & Total Number of Items Added to Inventory	(2) Total Cost to Add Inventory	(3) Cost per Item. Divide Column (2) by number in Column (1)	(4) No. Sold, Donated or Removed this year	(5) Value of All Inventory Removed. Column (3) x Column (4)	(6) Inventory Count at the End of the Tax Year	(7) Inv. Value at End of Year. Column (3) x Column (6)

NEW INVENTORY REPORT - page 2
(All new items added to inventory during tax year)

(1) Product & Total Number of Items Added to Inventory	(2) Total Cost to Add Inventory	(3) Cost per Item. Divide Column (2) by number in Column (1)	(4) No. Sold, Donated or Removed this year	(5) Value of All Inventory Removed. Column (3) x Column (4)	(6) Inventory Count at the End of the Tax Year	(7) Inv. Value at End of Year. Column (3) x Column (6)

NEW INVENTORY REPORT - page 3
(All new items added to inventory during tax year)

(1) Product & Total Number of Items Added to Inventory	(2) Total Cost to Add Inventory	(3) Cost per Item. Divide Column (2) by number in Column (1)	(4) No. Sold, Donated or Removed this year	(5) Value of All Inventory Removed. Column (3) x Column (4)	(6) Inventory Count at the End of the Tax Year	(7) Inv. Value at End of Year. Column (3) x Column (6)

Filling out a New Inventory Report

In Column (1) enter the Product Name and how many saleable items you initially added to your inventory.

Column (2) will include every penny you spent to produce or obtain that product. To get this figure you will add all of your material and production expenses together. Depending on the inventory item, you may have parts invoices, delivery expenses, outside labor, vendor invoices or other costs. Enter this total in Column (2).

The number in Column (3) is obtained by dividing the Total Cost (2) by Product Quantity (1).

In future years enter all new inventory on a New Inventory Report Sheet as it arrives, completing columns 1-3 at that time. You can fill out the rest of the columns on the last work day of the year, when you count the end of year inventory.

In Column (4) enter how many of this item were sold, given away as samples, destroyed or donated; in other words every item removed from your saleable inventory during the tax year. To determine this number complete your inventory count for Column (6) and subtract from the opening inventory count for the year.

Column (5) is figured by multiplying Column (3) x Column (4). That is the value assigned to all of the items sold this year, and will be the amount you get to deduct from your income.

Inventory is always counted on the last working day of the tax year. Simply count the items remaining in stock, both in your office as well as items unsold in a distributor's inventory, and enter that number in Column (6).

Column (7) is figured by multiplying Column (3) x Column (6).

Column (5) contains the total cost of items sold, and is the amount you can deduct from this year's inventory expense.

Creating a Prior Year Inventory Report

If this is not your first year with inventory you will also need a Prior Year Inventory Report for all inventory carried forward into the current tax year. On the next two pages you will find a blank Prior Year Inventory Report. Instructions follow.

PRIOR YEAR INVENTORY REPORT
(All inventory items carried forward to current tax year)

(1) Product/Number Remaining in Inventory at Beginning of Year	(2) Cost Per Item	(3) No. Sold, Donated or Removed from Inventory	(4) Value of Inventory Removed Column (2) x Column (3)	(5) Inventory Count at the End of Tax Year	(6) Value of Inventory At the End of Year Column (2) x Column (5)

PRIOR YEAR INVENTORY REPORT - page 2
(All inventory items carried forward to current tax year)

(1) Product/Number Remaining in Inventory at Beginning of Year	(2) Cost Per Item	(3) No. Sold, Donated or Removed from Inventory	(4) Value of Inventory Removed Column (2) x Column (3)	(5) Inventory Count at the End of Tax Year	(6) Value of Inventory At the End of Year Column (2) x Column (5)

Filling out a Prior Year Inventory Report

In Column (1) enter the Product Name and how many saleable items remained in inventory at the beginning of the tax year.

Column (2) is the same cost per item dollar amount you used to report inventory sold in prior years. Enter the Cost per Item in the second column.

The number in Column (3) reflects how many of this product you sold, gave away as samples, destroyed or donated. You can determine this figure by counting the inventory remaining at the end of the year and subtracting that from the opening inventory for the same year.

Column (4) is determined by multiplying Column (2) x Column (3). That is the total value assigned to all sales of this particular item, and will be the amount you get to deduct on your tax return.

On the last day of the tax year count all remaining inventory and enter that number in Column (5).

Column (6) is determined by multiplying Column (2) x Column (5). This is the total deductible value of inventory remaining unsold.

You'll learn how to deduct those inventory expenses in the next chapter. Once you have the details posted to the reports in this book, you can write new and prior year inventory totals on the front of the Inventory envelope, and put all inventory receipts inside. Set the Inventory envelope aside; you won't need it again unless you're audited.

PUTTING IT ALL TOGETHER

This final step has you posting all of the expense totals you've written on the front of the expense envelopes, along with some other necessary information you've already transferred to this book, onto a few final forms.

When you're done, this final report will contain all of the tax year information you or your tax professional will need in order to prepare your small business Schedule C tax return.

What to Take to the Tax Professional

A tax professional can only work from the information you provide and unless you know a little bit about business taxes even a good tax professional can easily miss valuable deductions.

<u>Tax Pro Rule #8</u>

**No matter how good your tax professional is,
if you don't provide
all of the necessary information and figures
your tax return will be wrong.**

You've already learned a lot, and by the time you finish this book you'll know enough to do your own simple Schedule C tax return if you choose. But, unless you have a thorough understanding of accounting it may not be the best thing for you to do, especially if you intend to depreciate your vehicle, home or new equipment.

Most people leave their tax professional's office each year knowing nothing more about IRS rules than they did the year before. When you visit your tax pro ask questions, and if he or she cannot answer your questions go elsewhere.

When you go for your annual tax appointment you'll want to take along all of your personal income tax information since a small business profit or loss is simply posted to your personal 1040 tax return before it is filed. Your tax professional will complete all of the supporting tax forms needed.

Have your taxes prepared as early in the year as possible. When you owe taxes the money is not due until April 15th, even if you mail your tax return on January 2nd. And remember, not all taxes are bad. Self-employment taxes fund your Social Security and Medicare, and if you don't pay much in while employed you won't draw much out during your senior years.

Deducting that Home Office

If you are planning on deducting your home office you'll need to take the following information to your tax preparer as well:

- Total square footage for your home. (This can be found in your home purchase or rental documents.)

- Total square footage of the area used exclusively for business. (Multiply the room length times the room width; if more than one room is used add those sums together.)

- Total annual amount paid for household insurance rent, repairs and lawn maintenance, utilities (electricity, water, sewer, gas, and garbage) and other household expenses that your home and business shared. If you had any expenses that were 100% home office related list those separately. You will also need your mortgage interest and real estate 1099's if you own your home.

Enter all of this information below:

_____ Total square footage of home

_____ Home office total square footage

$_____ Total of all shared utilities

List all home office expenses that were 100% business below:

If you choose to depreciate the home office portion of your home you should discuss this matter with a tax professional first.

Depreciating your home office could be a 30 year tax project, and when your home is eventually sold you will have to exclude the home office portion of gain from the personal residence tax shelter. Unless you understand the current tax laws on depreciation, this is not something individuals should tackle by themselves.

If you remodel your office or home, re-roof the structure, create a separate office entrance, or make any other changes that also affect the business portion of your home you can depreciate the business portion of those expenses as well. If you have any of these expenses be sure to include those along with the home office information on the prior page, and to discuss them with your tax professional.

Creating an Annual Tax Report

Your Annual Tax Report is where you combine your monthly totals to produce one end-of-year report. You've already done most of the work necessary.

This report is broken into three sections, Business Income, Business Expenses and Inventory Figures. In brief, you will:

1. Add up your monthly income to get the annual income total,

2. Add up your monthly expense report categories for annual expense totals, and

3. Complete the end of year columns on your inventory reports.

Business Income

You have already documented your business income in three places. The first is with your monthly bank statements, the second documentation came when you entered that monthly income onto the front of your Business Income Envelope, and the third when you transferred it to your Business Income End of Year Report Form.

If you have not already done so, put all of your monthly bank statements and checkbook registers into the Business Income Envelope.

Next, go to the Business Income End of Year Report on page 15-16 and transfer the Total Gross Income for the year onto the top of Your Annual Tax Report on page 54. We will be subtracting all of your business expenses and other costs from this before figuring the taxable amount.

Business Expenses

Because you have already sorted and grouped your business expenses into categories this next step will go quickly. Transfer the total from each envelope onto the matching line on Your Annual Tax Report next.

If you hire employees, have vehicle expenses or business mileage, or make any tax payments during the year you will also need to fill in some additional information on the following pages. Some of this will get you better tax breaks; other information will help you to survive a tax audit. Skip any items that do not apply to your business.

Payroll Expenses – If you hire employees you will need to bring all of your records for payroll expenses. These would include copies of your employees' W-2's as well as figures for total wages paid, social security taxes withheld as well as paid, federal and state income taxes withheld and paid for employees, plus any other money paid out for workman's comp, local taxes or unemployment insurance.

List those amounts below:

Vehicle & Mileage – Your preparer will need mileage and vehicle information on any vehicles that you used in your business. Whether you have one vehicle that you use exclusively for your business, or you use your family car for business errands, you still need to keep written records.

Start by listing each vehicle below:

Vehicle #1

Make & year:

Year first used in business:

Total miles driven this year in this car:

Business miles driven this year in this car:

Vehicle #2

Make & year:

Year first used in business:

Total miles driven this year in this car:

Business miles driven this year in this car:

If you have a vehicle reserved 100% for business use it is sometimes a better value to deduct actual expenses and depreciation on the business vehicle. If your vehicle is only for business use, list all out-of-pocket expenses paid or charged during the tax year on the following page.

Vehicle #1

Total amount spent for gasoline purchased:

Total repairs, and/or parts purchased:

Total car payments made (include price if you purchased a new vehicle this year), plus car insurance and all other expenses incurred for this vehicle. Itemize those items below:

Vehicle #2

Total amount spent for gasoline purchased:

Total repairs, and/or parts purchased:

Total car payments made (include price if you purchased a new vehicle this year), plus car insurance and all other expenses incurred for this vehicle. Itemize those items below:

Taxes – If you made quarterly tax payments you will need to list the total of all taxes paid below so that you can get credit on this year's tax return. You may be making payments both to the IRS and one or more states.

Also list any sales taxes, city taxes or other local taxes paid. Be sure to include the date each payment was made.

If you received W2-G tax forms take those with you to the tax preparer's office; let the preparer know that you have included these numbers with income and listed the total of all taxes deducted below.

- Federal Quarterly Tax Payments:

- State Quarterly Tax Payments:

- Other Business Taxes Paid:

- State & Federal Taxes Withheld on 1099's received:

Inventory – If you do not buy, make or purchase items for resale, you can skip this section. If you had inventory you will need to count your remaining inventory at the end of the tax year and enter your Opening Inventory, New Inventory Added, and Closing Inventory below.

Begin by counting all remaining inventory and completing your New and Prior Year Inventory Reports on pages 38-43. Once these reports are complete you can fill in the final inventory figures below.

Opening Inventory

If you had no inventory last year your opening inventory will be zero -- otherwise it will be the same dollar figure that you reported last year as your Closing Inventory. This should also be the total of your Prior Year Inventory.

Opening Inventory Value for current tax year: $_____.

New Inventory Added

To get the value of all new Inventory added simply total everything in column 2 on the New Inventory Report forms on page 38. This is the total amount you spent to acquire your new inventory during the tax year.

New Inventory Value added during current tax year: $_____.

Closing Inventory

Your Closing Inventory for this tax year is calculated by adding everything in the last column on all copies of both the New and Prior Year Inventory Reports. Fill in the total figure below:

Closing Inventory Value for current tax year: $_____.

THE ANNUAL TAX REPORT

A small business owner is allowed to set up a business retirement account, letting them divert a percentage of their profits for their own retirement, paying the taxes later when they expect lower earnings. A tax accountant can explain which account you qualify for and how much you can add each year.

The chapter title *Developing an Audit-Proof Mindset* explains what to do with all of those receipts and tax records you've organized, and how to think in a manner that will help you to avoid attracting an audit.

If you have not already done so transfer the total of all monthly expense categories for the entire tax year onto the three-page report that follows. If you need additional information it too will be found on the outside of your expense envelopes.

YOUR ANNUAL TAX REPORT FORM (20__)

Total Gross Income $_____

TOTAL ANNUAL EXPENSES

A - Advertising & Promotional Expenses $_____

B - Bank/Visa/Other Business Interest Paid $_____

C - Cleaning Materials & Business Supplies $_____

D - Donations to Nonprofit Organizations $_____

E - Educational Seminars & Classes $_____

F - Fix-it & Repair Expenses $_____

G - Gifts $_____

H - Home Office Expenses:

  Breakdown:

   Mortgage principle:

   Property tax:

   Insurance:

   Utilities and other shared expenses:

I - Insurance $_____

J - Job Required Licenses & Dues $_____

L - Legal & Professional Fees $_____

M - Meals & Entertainment: Total dollars $_____

N - Newspapers, Magazines & Subscriptions $_____

O - Office Supplies $_____

P - People Who Take a Share $_____

Q - Equipment Purchased $_____

Breakdown: List all new equipment, date purchased and amount spent below.

R - Rent Paid $_____

S - Shipping & Postage $_____

T - Travel: Non-meal Expenses $_____

For travel meals remember to include the number of nights away from home.

U - Utilities $_____   (do not include home office utilities here)

V - Vehicle (Car & Truck) Total Expenses $_____

Breakdown #1: Total business miles on calendar

Breakdown #2: List all vehicle expenses if you are depreciating a vehicle

W - Wages & Contract Labor Expenses $_____

Breakdown: W-2 and 1099 worker costs.

X - Taxes & Business Licenses $_____

Z - Inventory – YES or NO

This is the bulk of the information that you or your tax professional will need in order to add your self-employed business tax return to your personal 1040.

If you paid any taxes in advance, generally referred to as Estimated Quarterly Taxes, to either the state or federal government don't forget to include the date and amount paid for each of those payments. These quarterly payments are credited toward taxes due with your 1040 personal return.

If you have payroll expenses take all of your payroll reports and copies of any payroll tax forms filed with you when you visit your tax professional. Stick all of this paperwork in the back of this book so you'll have it all together when you need it.

If you have a simple business return, and always prepare your own personal tax return, the following chapter on preparing your own Schedule C tax return will help. It walks you through the process line-by-line, showing you where to post all of the information that you have entered on your Annual Tax Report.

No one without accounting knowledge should attempt a tax return with depreciation but anyone can figure the Section 179 expense deduction.

Equipment with a longer life than one year must be tracked for the lifetime of the item, and has complicated rules; and that is why depreciation is best left for tax professionals and accountants. But, unless it cost you hundreds of thousands of dollars you can still write this equipment off all at once.

The majority of independent contractors take depreciation deductions all at once by using the Section 179 deduction. This book explains how to take the Section 179 option, deducting the entire expense during the year of purchase.

If you want to depreciate your car or truck, instead of taking the standard mileage deduction, you are also no longer preparing a simple tax return. Depreciation is confusing, even for tax professionals, and the rules change often.

Vehicle depreciation instructions are not included in this guide. However, the standard mileage deduction includes depreciation.

This book's chapter on *Developing an Audit-Proof Mindset* explains what to do with all of the tax records you've organized, and how to think in a manner that will help you to avoid and win a tax audit.

The next chapter is for the entrepreneur or small business owner who prepares their own annual tax return. It walks you through the small business Schedule C tax form as well as supporting forms. If you do not intend to do your own taxes you can skip the next chapter.

PREPARING YOUR OWN SMALL BUSINESS TAX RETURN

Not everyone should be preparing their own taxes. Even those who are qualified would be smart to make an appointment with a tax professional for advice on tax planning every 3-5 years, just to learn what's new.

Any time you experience major changes in your business or personal life, you should consult with a tax professional for guidance. Making major decisions without considering the tax consequences can be expensive.

The following example is just one of the many common scenarios that can cost you money, if you don't know the current tax laws.

Example: Mary has held her job with a large corporation for the past 15 years, and now has the opportunity to buy the home she has been renting for the last 6 years. It would be her first home. The price is right; she has her down payment in the bank, and wants to close the deal.

Mary really wants to buy the house but she is also worried because once she empties her savings account for the down payment, she will have nothing to draw from in case of an emergency.

If Mary sat down with a tax professional his or her first question would probably be … do you have any retirement funds with the corporation that employs you, or an IRA that you can tap?

That's because the tax pro knows that retirement accounts can be used as down payment for first-time home buyers, without paying the 10% Early Withdrawal Penalty. That means Mary can leave her cash in the bank, and tap her retirement account for the down payment.

With proper planning, Mary might even be able to offset most of the federal and state income taxes owed when retirement money is withdrawn.

Buying the property in early January, and paying attention to how the sale is structured, can get Mary a larger Schedule A deduction, cancelling out retirement income gains. Without talking to a tax professional Mary would never have known all of this.

Tax Pro Rule #9

**Tax laws change every year,
sometimes offering huge tax savings for
only a short time. Even if you do your own taxes,
it is wise to speak with a tax pro occasionally,
just to keep up on new tax credits
and tax planning opportunities.**

When you prepare your own small business tax return you generally use the following five IRS forms:

- Schedule C - Profit or Loss from Business

- Schedule SE - Self-Employment Tax

- Form 4562 - Depreciation and Amortization

- Form 8829 - Expenses for Business Use of Your Home

- Form 1040 - U.S. Individual Income Tax (Long) Form

Although many IRS tax forms remain the same for years, the year at the top always changes. You can download forms for any recent tax year at www.IRS.gov. If you are preparing a prior year tax return you will need to download forms and instructions for that particular year.

The forms on the following pages represent those used in 2015 for the 2014 tax season. They are printed here so that you can become familiar with their format. These are the same forms used on the small portions that appear throughout this chapter.

SCHEDULE C
(Form 1040)

Department of the Treasury
Internal Revenue Service (99)

Profit or Loss From Business
(Sole Proprietorship)

▶ Information about Schedule C and its separate instructions is at www.irs.gov/schedulec.
▶ Attach to Form 1040, 1040NR, or 1041; partnerships generally must file Form 1065.

OMB No. 1545-0074

2014

Attachment
Sequence No. **09**

Name of proprietor

Social security number (SSN)

A	Principal business or profession, including product or service (see instructions)	**B** Enter code from instructions ▶
C	Business name. If no separate business name, leave blank.	**D** Employer ID number (EIN), (see instr.)

E Business address (including suite or room no.) ▶ ....
City, town or post office, state, and ZIP code

F Accounting method: **(1)** ☐ Cash **(2)** ☐ Accrual **(3)** ☐ Other (specify) ▶ ....

G Did you "materially participate" in the operation of this business during 2014? If "No," see instructions for limit on losses ☐ Yes ☐ No

H If you started or acquired this business during 2014, check here . . . . ▶ ☐

I Did you make any payments in 2014 that would require you to file Form(s) 1099? (see instructions) . . . ☐ Yes ☐ No

J If "Yes," did you or will you file required Forms 1099? . . . . ☐ Yes ☐ No

Part I   Income

1	Gross receipts or sales. See instructions for line 1 and check the box if this income was reported to you on Form W-2 and the "Statutory employee" box on that form was checked . . . . ▶ ☐	1	
2	Returns and allowances	2	
3	Subtract line 2 from line 1	3	
4	Cost of goods sold (from line 42)	4	
5	**Gross profit.** Subtract line 4 from line 3	5	
6	Other income, including federal and state gasoline or fuel tax credit or refund (see instructions) . . .	6	
7	**Gross income.** Add lines 5 and 6 . . . . ▶	7	

Part II   Expenses. Enter expenses for business use of your home only on line 30.

8	Advertising	8		18	Office expense (see instructions)	18
9	Car and truck expenses (see instructions)	9		19	Pension and profit-sharing plans .	19
				20	Rent or lease (see instructions):	
10	Commissions and fees .	10		a	Vehicles, machinery, and equipment	20a
11	Contract labor (see instructions)	11		b	Other business property . . .	20b
12	Depletion	12		21	Repairs and maintenance . . .	21
13	Depreciation and section 179 expense deduction (not included in Part III) (see instructions)	13		22	Supplies (not included in Part III) .	22
				23	Taxes and licenses	23
				24	Travel, meals, and entertainment:	
14	Employee benefit programs (other than on line 19) . .	14		a	Travel	24a
15	Insurance (other than health)	15		b	Deductible meals and entertainment (see instructions) .	24b
16	Interest:			25	Utilities	25
a	Mortgage (paid to banks, etc.)	16a		26	Wages (less employment credits) .	26
b	Other	16b		27a	Other expenses (from line 48) . .	27a
17	Legal and professional services	17		b	Reserved for future use . . .	27b

28	**Total expenses** before expenses for business use of home. Add lines 8 through 27a . . . . . ▶	28	
29	Tentative profit or (loss). Subtract line 28 from line 7	29	
30	Expenses for business use of your home. Do not report these expenses elsewhere. Attach Form 8829 unless using the simplified method (see instructions). **Simplified method filers only:** enter the total square footage of: (a) your home: _____ and (b) the part of your home used for business: _____ . Use the Simplified Method Worksheet in the instructions to figure the amount to enter on line 30	30	
31	**Net profit or (loss).** Subtract line 30 from line 29. • If a profit, enter on both **Form 1040, line 12** (or **Form 1040NR, line 13**) and on **Schedule SE, line 2.** (If you checked the box on line 1, see instructions). Estates and trusts, enter on **Form 1041, line 3.** • If a loss, you **must** go to line 32.	31	
32	If you have a loss, check the box that describes your investment in this activity (see instructions). • If you checked 32a, enter the loss on both **Form 1040, line 12,** (or **Form 1040NR, line 13**) and on **Schedule SE, line 2.** (If you checked the box on line 1, see the line 31 instructions). Estates and trusts, enter on **Form 1041, line 3.** • If you checked 32b, you **must** attach Form 6198. Your loss may be limited.	32a ☐ All investment is at risk. 32b ☐ Some investment is not at risk.	

For Paperwork Reduction Act Notice, see the separate instructions.   Cat. No. 11334P   Schedule C (Form 1040) 2014

Schedule C (Form 1040) 2014

Page **2**

Part III Cost of Goods Sold (see instructions)

33 Method(s) used to value closing inventory: a ☐ Cost b ☐ Lower of cost or market c ☐ Other (attach explanation)

34 Was there any change in determining quantities, costs, or valuations between opening and closing inventory?
If "Yes," attach explanation . . . . ☐ Yes ☐ No

35 Inventory at beginning of year. If different from last year's closing inventory, attach explanation	35	
36 Purchases less cost of items withdrawn for personal use	36	
37 Cost of labor. Do not include any amounts paid to yourself	37	
38 Materials and supplies	38	
39 Other costs	39	
40 Add lines 35 through 39	40	
41 Inventory at end of year	41	
42 **Cost of goods sold.** Subtract line 41 from line 40. Enter the result here and on line 4	42	

Part IV Information on Your Vehicle. Complete this part **only** if you are claiming car or truck expenses on line 9 and are not required to file Form 4562 for this business. See the instructions for line 13 to find out if you must file Form 4562.

43 When did you place your vehicle in service for business purposes? (month, day, year) ▶ ___ / ___ / ___

44 Of the total number of miles you drove your vehicle during 2014, enter the number of miles you used your vehicle for:

a Business _____ b Commuting (see instructions) _____ c Other _____

45 Was your vehicle available for personal use during off-duty hours? . . . . ☐ Yes ☐ No

46 Do you (or your spouse) have another vehicle available for personal use? . . . . ☐ Yes ☐ No

47a Do you have evidence to support your deduction? . . . . ☐ Yes ☐ No

  b If "Yes," is the evidence written? . . . . ☐ Yes ☐ No

Part V Other Expenses. List below business expenses not included on lines 8–26 or line 30.

....	
....	
....	
....	
....	
....	
....	
....	
....	

48 Total other expenses. Enter here and on line 27a . . . . | 48 | |

Schedule C (Form 1040) 2014

SCHEDULE SE
(Form 1040)

Department of the Treasury
Internal Revenue Service (99)

Self-Employment Tax

▶ Information about Schedule SE and its separate instructions is at www.irs.gov/schedulese.
▶ Attach to Form 1040 or Form 1040NR.

OMB No. 1545-0074

20**14**

Attachment
Sequence No. **17**

Name of person with **self-employment** income (as shown on Form 1040 or Form 1040NR)

Social security number of person
with **self-employment** income ▶

Before you begin: To determine if you must file Schedule SE, see the instructions.

May I Use Short Schedule SE or Must I Use Long Schedule SE?

Note. Use this flowchart **only** if you must file Schedule SE. If unsure, see *Who Must File Schedule SE* in the instructions.

Section A—Short Schedule SE. Caution. Read above to see if you can use Short Schedule SE.

1a Net farm profit or (loss) from Schedule F, line 34, and farm partnerships, Schedule K-1 (Form 1065), box 14, code A	**1a**	
b If you received social security retirement or disability benefits, enter the amount of Conservation Reserve Program payments included on Schedule F, line 4b, or listed on Schedule K-1 (Form 1065), box 20, code Z	**1b** (	)
2 Net profit or (loss) from Schedule C, line 31; Schedule C-EZ, line 3; Schedule K-1 (Form 1065), box 14, code A (other than farming); and Schedule K-1 (Form 1065-B), box 9, code J1. Ministers and members of religious orders, see instructions for types of income to report on this line. See instructions for other income to report	**2**	
3 Combine lines 1a, 1b, and 2	**3**	
4 Multiply line 3 by 92.35% (.9235). If less than $400, you do not owe self-employment tax; **do not file this schedule unless you have an amount on line 1b** . . . . ▶	**4**	
Note. If line 4 is less than $400 due to Conservation Reserve Program payments on line 1b, see instructions.		
5 **Self-employment tax.** If the amount on line 4 is: • $117,000 or less, multiply line 4 by 15.3% (.153). Enter the result here and on **Form 1040, line 57,** or **Form 1040NR, line 55** • More than $117,000, multiply line 4 by 2.9% (.029). Then, add $14,508 to the result. Enter the total here and on **Form 1040, line 57, or Form 1040NR, line 55**	**5**	
6 **Deduction for one-half of self-employment tax.** Multiply line 5 by 50% (.50). Enter the result here and on **Form 1040, line 27, or Form 1040NR, line 27** **6**		

For Paperwork Reduction Act Notice, see your tax return instructions.   Cat. No. 11358Z   Schedule SE (Form 1040) 2014

Schedule SE (Form 1040) 2014   Attachment Sequence No. **17**   Page **2**

Name of person with **self-employment** income (as shown on Form 1040 or Form 1040NR)	Social security number of person with **self-employment** income ▶

Section B — Long Schedule SE

Part I   Self-Employment Tax

Note. If your only income subject to self-employment tax is **church employee income**, see instructions. Also see instructions for the definition of church employee income.

A   If you are a minister, member of a religious order, or Christian Science practitioner **and** you filed Form 4361, but you had $400 or more of **other** net earnings from self-employment, check here and continue with Part I . . . . ▶ ☐

1a   Net farm profit or (loss) from Schedule F, line 34, and farm partnerships, Schedule K-1 (Form 1065), box 14, code A. **Note.** Skip lines 1a and 1b if you use the farm optional method (see instructions)   **1a**

    b   If you received social security retirement or disability benefits, enter the amount of Conservation Reserve Program payments included on Schedule F, line 4b, or listed on Schedule K-1 (Form 1065), box 20, code Z   **1b** (   )

2   Net profit or (loss) from Schedule C, line 31; Schedule C-EZ, line 3; Schedule K-1 (Form 1065), box 14, code A (other than farming); and Schedule K-1 (Form 1065-B), box 9, code J1. Ministers and members of religious orders, see instructions for types of income to report on this line. See instructions for other income to report. **Note.** Skip this line if you use the nonfarm optional method (see instructions) **2**

3   Combine lines 1a, 1b, and 2 . . . . **3**

4a   If line 3 is more than zero, multiply line 3 by 92.35% (.9235). Otherwise, enter amount from line 3   **4a**
     Note. If line 4a is less than $400 due to Conservation Reserve Program payments on line 1b, see instructions.

    b   If you elect one or both of the optional methods, enter the total of lines 15 and 17 here . .   **4b**

    c   Combine lines 4a and 4b. If less than $400, **stop;** you do not owe self-employment tax.
     Exception. If less than $400 and you had **church employee income,** enter -0- and continue ▶   **4c**

5a   Enter your **church employee income** from Form W-2. See instructions for definition of church employee income . . . **5a**

    b   Multiply line 5a by 92.35% (.9235). If less than $100, enter -0- **5b**

6   Add lines 4c and 5b **6**

7   Maximum amount of combined wages and self-employment earnings subject to social security tax or the 6.2% portion of the 7.65% railroad retirement (tier 1) tax for 2014 . . . . . .   **7**   117,000 | 00

8a   Total social security wages and tips (total of boxes 3 and 7 on Form(s) W-2) and railroad retirement (tier 1) compensation. If $117,000 or more, skip lines 8b through 10, and go to line 11   **8a**

    b   Unreported tips subject to social security tax (from Form 4137, line 10)   **8b**

    c   Wages subject to social security tax (from Form 8919, line 10)   **8c**

    d   Add lines 8a, 8b, and 8c **8d**

9   Subtract line 8d from line 7. If zero or less, enter -0- here and on line 10 and go to line 11 . ▶   **9**

10   Multiply the **smaller** of line 6 or line 9 by 12.4% (.124) **10**

11   Multiply line 6 by 2.9% (.029) **11**

12   **Self-employment tax.** Add lines 10 and 11. Enter here and on **Form 1040, line 57,** or **Form 1040NR, line 55**   **12**

13   Deduction for one-half of self-employment tax.
     Multiply line 12 by 50% (.50). Enter the result here and on
     Form 1040, line 27, or **Form 1040NR, line 27** **13**

Part II   Optional Methods To Figure Net Earnings (see instructions)

Farm Optional Method. You may use this method **only if (a)** your gross farm income[1] was not more than $7,200, **or (b)** your net farm profits[2] were less than $5,198.

14   Maximum income for optional methods . . . . **14**   4,800 | 00

15   Enter the **smaller of:** two-thirds (⅔) of gross farm income[1] (not less than zero) **or** $4,800. Also include this amount on line 4b above **15**

Nonfarm Optional Method. You may use this method **only if (a)** your net nonfarm profits[3] were less than $5,198 and also less than 72.189% of your gross nonfarm income,[4] **and (b)** you had net earnings from self-employment of at least $400 in 2 of the prior 3 years. **Caution.** You may use this method no more than five times.

16   Subtract line 15 from line 14 . . . . **16**

17   Enter the **smaller of:** two-thirds (⅔) of gross nonfarm income[4] (not less than zero) or the amount on line 16. Also include this amount on line 4b above **17**

[1] From Sch. F, line 9, and Sch. K-1 (Form 1065), box 14, code B.
[2] From Sch. F, line 34, and Sch. K-1 (Form 1065), box 14, code A—minus the amount you would have entered on line 1b had you not used the optional method.

[3] From Sch. C, line 31; Sch. C-EZ, line 3; Sch. K-1 (Form 1065), box 14, code A; and Sch. K-1 (Form 1065-B), box 9, code J1.
[4] From Sch. C, line 7; Sch. C-EZ, line 1; Sch. K-1 (Form 1065), box 14, code C; and Sch. K-1 (Form 1065-B), box 9, code J2.

Schedule SE (Form 1040) 2014

Form 4562

Department of the Treasury
Internal Revenue Service (99)

Depreciation and Amortization
(Including Information on Listed Property)
▶ Attach to your tax return.
▶ Information about Form 4562 and its separate instructions is at www.irs.gov/form4562.

OMB No. 1545-0172

2014

Attachment
Sequence No. **179**

Name(s) shown on return | Business or activity to which this form relates | Identifying number

Part I — Election To Expense Certain Property Under Section 179
Note: If you have any listed property, complete Part V before you complete Part I.

1	Maximum amount (see instructions)	**1**
2	Total cost of section 179 property placed in service (see instructions)	**2**
3	Threshold cost of section 179 property before reduction in limitation (see instructions) . . .	**3**
4	Reduction in limitation. Subtract line 3 from line 2. If zero or less, enter -0-	**4**
5	Dollar limitation for tax year. Subtract line 4 from line 1. If zero or less, enter -0-. If married filing separately, see instructions	**5**

6	(a) Description of property	(b) Cost (business use only)	(c) Elected cost

7	Listed property. Enter the amount from line 29 . . . . **7**	
8	Total elected cost of section 179 property. Add amounts in column (c), lines 6 and 7	**8**
9	Tentative deduction. Enter the **smaller** of line 5 or line 8	**9**
10	Carryover of disallowed deduction from line 13 of your 2013 Form 4562	**10**
11	Business income limitation. Enter the smaller of business income (not less than zero) or line 5 (see instructions)	**11**
12	Section 179 expense deduction. Add lines 9 and 10, but do not enter more than line 11	**12**
13	Carryover of disallowed deduction to 2015. Add lines 9 and 10, less line 12 ▶ **13**	

Note: Do not use Part II or Part III below for listed property. Instead, use Part V.

Part II — Special Depreciation Allowance and Other Depreciation (Do not include listed property.) (See instructions.)

14	Special depreciation allowance for qualified property (other than listed property) placed in service during the tax year (see instructions)	**14**
15	Property subject to section 168(f)(1) election	**15**
16	Other depreciation (including ACRS)	**16**

Part III — MACRS Depreciation (Do not include listed property.) (See instructions.)

Section A

17	MACRS deductions for assets placed in service in tax years beginning before 2014	**17**
18	If you are electing to group any assets placed in service during the tax year into one or more general asset accounts, check here . . . . ▶ ☐	

Section B — Assets Placed in Service During 2014 Tax Year Using the General Depreciation System

(a) Classification of property	(b) Month and year placed in service	(c) Basis for depreciation (business/investment use only — see instructions)	(d) Recovery period	(e) Convention	(f) Method	(g) Depreciation deduction
19a 3-year property						
b 5-year property						
c 7-year property						
d 10-year property						
e 15-year property						
f 20-year property						
g 25-year property			25 yrs.		S/L	
h Residential rental property			27.5 yrs.	MM	S/L	
			27.5 yrs.	MM	S/L	
i Nonresidential real property			39 yrs.	MM	S/L	
				MM	S/L	

Section C — Assets Placed in Service During 2014 Tax Year Using the Alternative Depreciation System

20a Class life					S/L	
b 12-year			12 yrs.		S/L	
c 40-year			40 yrs.	MM	S/L	

Part IV — Summary (See instructions.)

21	Listed property. Enter amount from line 28	**21**
22	**Total.** Add amounts from line 12, lines 14 through 17, lines 19 and 20 in column (g), and line 21. Enter here and on the appropriate lines of your return. Partnerships and S corporations—see instructions .	**22**
23	For assets shown above and placed in service during the current year, enter the portion of the basis attributable to section 263A costs **23**	

For Paperwork Reduction Act Notice, see separate instructions. — Cat. No. 12906N — Form **4562** (2014)

Form 4562 (2014)

Page **2**

Part V — Listed Property (Include automobiles, certain other vehicles, certain aircraft, certain computers, and property used for entertainment, recreation, or amusement.)

Note: For any vehicle for which you are using the standard mileage rate or deducting lease expense, complete only 24a, 24b, columns (a) through (c) of Section A, all of Section B, and Section C if applicable.

Section A—Depreciation and Other Information (Caution: See the instructions for limits for passenger automobiles.)

24a Do you have evidence to support the business/investment use claimed? ☐ Yes ☐ No   24b If "Yes," is the evidence written? ☐ Yes ☐ No

(a) Type of property (list vehicles first)	(b) Date placed in service	(c) Business/investment use percentage	(d) Cost or other basis	(e) Basis for depreciation (business/investment use only)	(f) Recovery period	(g) Method/Convention	(h) Depreciation deduction	(i) Elected section 179 cost
25 Special depreciation allowance for qualified listed property placed in service during the tax year and used more than 50% in a qualified business use (see instructions) . **25**								
26 Property used more than 50% in a qualified business use:								
		%						
		%						
		%						
27 Property used 50% or less in a qualified business use:								
		%				S/L –		
		%				S/L –		
		%				S/L –		
28 Add amounts in column (h), lines 25 through 27. Enter here and on line 21, page 1 . **28**								
29 Add amounts in column (i), line 26. Enter here and on line 7, page 1 . . . . **29**								

Section B—Information on Use of Vehicles

Complete this section for vehicles used by a sole proprietor, partner, or other "more than 5% owner," or related person. If you provided vehicles to your employees, first answer the questions in Section C to see if you meet an exception to completing this section for those vehicles.

	(a) Vehicle 1		(b) Vehicle 2		(c) Vehicle 3		(d) Vehicle 4		(e) Vehicle 5		(f) Vehicle 6	
30 Total business/investment miles driven during the year (do not include commuting miles) .												
31 Total commuting miles driven during the year												
32 Total other personal (noncommuting) miles driven												
33 Total miles driven during the year. Add lines 30 through 32												
34 Was the vehicle available for personal use during off-duty hours?	Yes	No	Yes	No	Yes	No	Yes	No	Yes	No	Yes	No
35 Was the vehicle used primarily by a more than 5% owner or related person? . .												
36 Is another vehicle available for personal use?												

Section C—Questions for Employers Who Provide Vehicles for Use by Their Employees

Answer these questions to determine if you meet an exception to completing Section B for vehicles used by employees who are **not** more than 5% owners or related persons (see instructions).

	Yes	No
37 Do you maintain a written policy statement that prohibits all personal use of vehicles, including commuting, by your employees? . . .		
38 Do you maintain a written policy statement that prohibits personal use of vehicles, except commuting, by your employees? See the instructions for vehicles used by corporate officers, directors, or 1% or more owners . .		
39 Do you treat all use of vehicles by employees as personal use?		
40 Do you provide more than five vehicles to your employees, obtain information from your employees about the use of the vehicles, and retain the information received?		
41 Do you meet the requirements concerning qualified automobile demonstration use? (See instructions.) . . .		

Note: If your answer to 37, 38, 39, 40, or 41 is "Yes," do not complete Section B for the covered vehicles.

Part VI — Amortization

(a) Description of costs	(b) Date amortization begins	(c) Amortizable amount	(d) Code section	(e) Amortization period or percentage	(f) Amortization for this year
42 Amortization of costs that begins during your 2014 tax year (see instructions):					
43 Amortization of costs that began before your 2014 tax year **43**					
44 Total. Add amounts in column (f). See the instructions for where to report **44**					

Form **4562** (2014)

Form 8829

Department of the Treasury
Internal Revenue Service (99)

Expenses for Business Use of Your Home

▶ File only with Schedule C (Form 1040). Use a separate Form 8829 for each home you used for business during the year.
▶ Information about Form 8829 and its separate instructions is at *www.irs.gov/form8829.*

OMB No. 1545-0074

2014

Attachment
Sequence No. **176**

Name(s) of proprietor(s)

Your social security number

Part I — Part of Your Home Used for Business

1	Area used regularly and exclusively for business, regularly for daycare, or for storage of inventory or product samples (see instructions)	1	
2	Total area of home	2	
3	Divide line 1 by line 2. Enter the result as a percentage	3	%

For daycare facilities not used exclusively for business, go to line 4. All others, go to line 7.

4	Multiply days used for daycare during year by hours used per day	4	hr.
5	Total hours available for use during the year (365 days x 24 hours) (see instructions)	5	8,760 hr.
6	Divide line 4 by line 5. Enter the result as a decimal amount	6	.
7	Business percentage. For daycare facilities not used exclusively for business, multiply line 6 by line 3 (enter the result as a percentage). All others, enter the amount from line 3 ▶	7	%

Part II — Figure Your Allowable Deduction

		(a) Direct expenses	(b) Indirect expenses	
8	Enter the amount from Schedule C, line 29, **plus** any gain derived from the business use of your home, **minus** any loss from the trade or business not derived from the business use of your home (see instructions)			8
	See instructions for **columns (a) and (b) before completing lines 9–21.**			
9	Casualty losses (see instructions)	9		
10	Deductible mortgage interest (see instructions)	10		
11	Real estate taxes (see instructions)	11		
12	Add lines 9, 10, and 11	12		
13	Multiply line 12, column (b) by line 7		13	
14	Add line 12, column (a) and line 13			14
15	Subtract line 14 from line 8. If zero or less, enter -0-			15
16	Excess mortgage interest (see instructions)	16		
17	Insurance	17		
18	Rent	18		
19	Repairs and maintenance	19		
20	Utilities	20		
21	Other expenses (see instructions)	21		
22	Add lines 16 through 21	22		
23	Multiply line 22, column (b) by line 7		23	
24	Carryover of prior year operating expenses (see instructions)		24	
25	Add line 22, column (a), line 23, and line 24			25
26	Allowable operating expenses. Enter the **smaller** of line 15 or line 25			26
27	Limit on excess casualty losses and depreciation. Subtract line 26 from line 15			27
28	Excess casualty losses (see instructions)		28	
29	Depreciation of your home from line 41 below		29	
30	Carryover of prior year excess casualty losses and depreciation (see instructions)		30	
31	Add lines 28 through 30			31
32	Allowable excess casualty losses and depreciation. Enter the **smaller** of line 27 or line 31			32
33	Add lines 14, 26, and 32			33
34	Casualty loss portion, if any, from lines 14 and 32. Carry amount to **Form 4684** (see instructions)			34
35	**Allowable expenses for business use of your home.** Subtract line 34 from line 33. Enter here and on Schedule C, line 30. If your home was used for more than one business, see instructions ▶			35

Part III — Depreciation of Your Home

36	Enter the **smaller** of your home's adjusted basis or its fair market value (see instructions)	36	
37	Value of land included on line 36	37	
38	Basis of building. Subtract line 37 from line 36	38	
39	Business basis of building. Multiply line 38 by line 7	39	
40	Depreciation percentage (see instructions)	40	%
41	Depreciation allowable (see instructions). Multiply line 39 by line 40. Enter here and on line 29 above	41	

Part IV — Carryover of Unallowed Expenses to 2015

42	Operating expenses. Subtract line 26 from line 25. If less than zero, enter -0-	42	
43	Excess casualty losses and depreciation. Subtract line 32 from line 31. If less than zero, enter -0-	43	

For Paperwork Reduction Act Notice, see your tax return instructions.

Cat. No. 13232M

Form **8829** (2014)

67

Form 1040 Department of the Treasury—Internal Revenue Service (99)
U.S. Individual Income Tax Return **2014** OMB No. 1545-0074 IRS Use Only—Do not write or staple in this space.

For the year Jan. 1–Dec. 31, 2014, or other tax year beginning , 2014, ending , 20 | See separate instructions.

Your first name and initial | Last name | Your social security number

If a joint return, spouse's first name and initial | Last name | Spouse's social security number

Home address (number and street). If you have a P.O. box, see instructions. | Apt. no. | ▲ Make sure the SSN(s) above and on line 6c are correct.

City, town or post office, state, and ZIP code. If you have a foreign address, also complete spaces below (see instructions).

Presidential Election Campaign
Check here if you, or your spouse if filing jointly, want $3 to go to this fund. Checking a box below will not change your tax or refund. ☐ You ☐ Spouse

Foreign country name | Foreign province/state/county | Foreign postal code

Filing Status
Check only one box.

1 ☐ Single
2 ☐ Married filing jointly (even if only one had income)
3 ☐ Married filing separately. Enter spouse's SSN above and full name here. ▶
4 ☐ Head of household (with qualifying person). (See instructions.) If the qualifying person is a child but not your dependent, enter this child's name here. ▶
5 ☐ Qualifying widow(er) with dependent child

Exemptions

6a ☐ Yourself. If someone can claim you as a dependent, do not check box 6a
b ☐ Spouse

c Dependents:		(2) Dependent's social security number	(3) Dependent's relationship to you	(4) ✓ if child under age 17 qualifying for child tax credit (see instructions)
(1) First name Last name				
				☐
				☐
				☐
				☐

If more than four dependents, see instructions and check here ▶ ☐

Boxes checked on 6a and 6b
No. of children on 6c who:
• lived with you
• did not live with you due to divorce or separation (see instructions)
Dependents on 6c not entered above
Add numbers on lines above ▶

d Total number of exemptions claimed

Income

Attach Form(s) W-2 here. Also attach Forms W-2G and 1099-R if tax was withheld.

If you did not get a W-2, see instructions.

7 Wages, salaries, tips, etc. Attach Form(s) W-2 | 7
8a Taxable interest. Attach Schedule B if required | 8a
b Tax-exempt interest. Do not include on line 8a | 8b
9a Ordinary dividends. Attach Schedule B if required | 9a
b Qualified dividends | 9b
10 Taxable refunds, credits, or offsets of state and local income taxes | 10
11 Alimony received | 11
12 Business income or (loss). Attach Schedule C or C-EZ | 12
13 Capital gain or (loss). Attach Schedule D if required. If not required, check here ▶ ☐ | 13
14 Other gains or (losses). Attach Form 4797 | 14
15a IRA distributions 15a | b Taxable amount | 15b
16a Pensions and annuities 16a | b Taxable amount | 16b
17 Rental real estate, royalties, partnerships, S corporations, trusts, etc. Attach Schedule E | 17
18 Farm income or (loss). Attach Schedule F | 18
19 Unemployment compensation | 19
20a Social security benefits 20a | b Taxable amount | 20b
21 Other income. List type and amount | 21
22 Combine the amounts in the far right column for lines 7 through 21. This is your **total income** ▶ | 22

Adjusted Gross Income

23 Educator expenses | 23
24 Certain business expenses of reservists, performing artists, and fee-basis government officials. Attach Form 2106 or 2106-EZ | 24
25 Health savings account deduction. Attach Form 8889 | 25
26 Moving expenses. Attach Form 3903 | 26
27 Deductible part of self-employment tax. Attach Schedule SE | 27
28 Self-employed SEP, SIMPLE, and qualified plans | 28
29 Self-employed health insurance deduction | 29
30 Penalty on early withdrawal of savings | 30
31a Alimony paid b Recipient's SSN ▶ | 31a
32 IRA deduction | 32
33 Student loan interest deduction | 33
34 Tuition and fees. Attach Form 8917 | 34
35 Domestic production activities deduction. Attach Form 8903 | 35
36 Add lines 23 through 35 | 36
37 Subtract line 36 from line 22. This is your **adjusted gross income** ▶ | 37

For Disclosure, Privacy Act, and Paperwork Reduction Act Notice, see separate instructions. Cat. No. 11320B Form **1040** (2014)

Form 1040 (2014)   Page **2**

Tax and Credits	38	Amount from line 37 (adjusted gross income)		38
	39a	Check { ☐ **You** were born before January 2, 1950, ☐ Blind. } **Total boxes** ☐		
		{ ☐ **Spouse** was born before January 2, 1950, ☐ Blind. } **checked ►** 39a		
	b	If your spouse itemizes on a separate return or you were a dual-status alien, check here► 39b☐		
Standard Deduction for—	40	**Itemized deductions** (from Schedule A) or your **standard deduction** (see left margin)		40
	41	Subtract line 40 from line 38		41
• People who check any box on line 39a or 39b or who can be claimed as a dependent, see instructions.	42	**Exemptions.** If line 38 is $152,525 or less, multiply $3,950 by the number on line 6d. Otherwise, see instructions		42
	43	**Taxable income.** Subtract line 42 from line 41. If line 42 is more than line 41, enter -0-		43
	44	**Tax** (see instructions). Check if any from: **a** ☐ Form(s) 8814 **b** ☐ Form 4972 **c** ☐		44
	45	**Alternative minimum tax** (see instructions). Attach Form 6251		45
	46	Excess advance premium tax credit repayment. Attach Form 8962		46
• All others:	47	Add lines 44, 45, and 46 ►		47
Single or Married filing separately, $6,200	48	Foreign tax credit. Attach Form 1116 if required	48	
	49	Credit for child and dependent care expenses. Attach Form 2441	49	
Married filing jointly or Qualifying widow(er), $12,400	50	Education credits from Form 8863, line 19	50	
	51	Retirement savings contributions credit. Attach Form 8880	51	
	52	Child tax credit. Attach Schedule 8812, if required	52	
Head of household, $9,100	53	Residential energy credits. Attach Form 5695	53	
	54	Other credits from Form: **a** ☐ 3800 **b** ☐ 8801 **c** ☐	54	
	55	Add lines 48 through 54. These are your **total credits**		55
	56	Subtract line 55 from line 47. If line 55 is more than line 47, enter -0- ►		56
Other Taxes	57	Self-employment tax. Attach Schedule SE		57
	58	Unreported social security and Medicare tax from Form: **a** ☐ 4137 **b** ☐ 8919		58
	59	Additional tax on IRAs, other qualified retirement plans, etc. Attach Form 5329 if required		59
	60a	Household employment taxes from Schedule H		60a
	b	First-time homebuyer credit repayment. Attach Form 5405 if required		60b
	61	Health care: individual responsibility (see instructions) Full-year coverage ☐		61
	62	Taxes from: **a** ☐ Form 8959 **b** ☐ Form 8960 **c** ☐ Instructions; enter code(s)		62
	63	Add lines 56 through 62. This is your **total tax** ►		63
Payments	64	Federal income tax withheld from Forms W-2 and 1099	64	
	65	2014 estimated tax payments and amount applied from 2013 return	65	
If you have a qualifying child, attach Schedule EIC.	66a	**Earned income credit (EIC)**	66a	
	b	Nontaxable combat pay election 66b		
	67	Additional child tax credit. Attach Schedule 8812	67	
	68	American opportunity credit from Form 8863, line 8	68	
	69	Net premium tax credit. Attach Form 8962	69	
	70	Amount paid with request for extension to file	70	
	71	Excess social security and tier 1 RRTA tax withheld	71	
	72	Credit for federal tax on fuels. Attach Form 4136	72	
	73	Credits from Form: **a** ☐ 2439 **b** ☐ Reserved **c** ☐ Reserved **d** ☐	73	
	74	Add lines 64, 65, 66a, and 67 through 73. These are your **total payments** ►		74
Refund	75	If line 74 is more than line 63, subtract line 63 from line 74. This is the amount you **overpaid**		75
	76a	Amount of line 75 you want **refunded to you.** If Form 8888 is attached, check here ► ☐		76a
Direct deposit? ► See Instructions.	b	Routing number ▏▏▏▏▏▏▏▏▏ ►c Type: ☐ Checking ☐ Savings		
	d	Account number ▏▏▏▏▏▏▏▏▏▏▏▏▏		
	77	Amount of line 75 you want **applied to your 2015 estimated tax ►** 77		
Amount You Owe	78	**Amount you owe.** Subtract line 74 from line 63. For details on how to pay, see instructions ►		78
	79	Estimated tax penalty (see instructions) 79		
Third Party Designee		Do you want to allow another person to discuss this return with the IRS (see instructions)? ☐ **Yes.** Complete below. ☐ **No**		
		Designee's name ► ⸻ Phone no. ► ⸻ Personal identification number (PIN) ► ▏▏▏▏▏		

Sign Here
Joint return? See instructions.
Keep a copy for your records.

Under penalties of perjury, I declare that I have examined this return and accompanying schedules and statements, and to the best of my knowledge and belief, they are true, correct, and complete. Declaration of preparer (other than taxpayer) is based on all information of which preparer has any knowledge.

Your signature	Date	Your occupation	Daytime phone number
Spouse's signature. If a joint return, **both** must sign.	Date	Spouse's occupation	If the IRS sent you an Identity Protection PIN, enter it here (see inst.) ▏▏▏▏▏▏

Paid Preparer Use Only

Print/Type preparer's name	Preparer's signature	Date	Check ☐ if self-employed — PTIN
Firm's name ►			Firm's EIN ►
Firm's address ►			Phone no.

www.irs.gov/form1040   Form **1040** (2014)

Introducing Schedule C - The Small Business Tax Form

IRS Form Schedule C is where all small business income and expenses are reported. This tax form is not submitted separately, but is filed along with your personal tax return and the net profit or loss from this form is posted to your 1040 tax form.

Any individual or married couple operating a small business will use this form; corporations and un-married partnerships do not use this form.

If you have less than $5,000 worth of expenses, and they appear in only a couple of categories, you may be able to use Schedule C-EZ.

Small business owners who establish a corporate structure merely for financial protection may still end up filing their business taxes on IRS form Schedule C. Ask the professional who helped you to set up your corporation if you're not sure which form to file.

If you have more than one business, and they are not related, you will need to fill out more than one Schedule C. A barber who also sells hair gel can include all income and expenses on one Schedule C. A salon owner who also bakes cakes for a local bakery would need a separate Schedule C for the cake business.

This chapter is designed to walk you through the actual preparation of your Schedule C tax form, line-by-line.

All of the figures that you will need can be found on the reports you filled out in this book; it's just a matter of transferring that information as instructed.

Completing a Schedule C Tax Form

Schedule C, and any other tax forms you need, can be downloaded at www.IRS.gov. To get the current year's Schedule C first click on Forms and Publications, and then click on the Schedule C link to print or download.

The following pages will explain where to post all of the income, expenses and other details you wrote in this book. These instructions are written in a manner that allows you to sit down with your tax form and move line by line, dropping in numbers as directed.

Whenever you're supposed to write information on a particular line of your tax form, that line number or heading will be all in CAPITAL letters, to help you to focus on where you're supposed to write your information.

Instructions for supporting forms that you need to complete a *simple* business return have also been included.

Now let's work on that Schedule C, section by section. An illustration of the top portion appears below.

Begin by filling in the self-employed person's name in the box marked **PROPRIETOR**; put their **SOCIAL SECURITY NUMBER** in the box at the end of the line.

LINE A is where you will write your profession – barber, hair stylist or salon owner, followed by the business code for your industry.

You can actually enter any title that you feel fits what you do for a living best – beauty shop owner, cosmetologist, wedding hair stylist, or any other hair-care professional title you have chosen.

The code to write on **LINE B** is 812111 if you own or rent space in a barber shop. A barber shop generally caters to men.

The word barber does not need to be in the name of the shop for it to be classified as a barber shop. If your shop offers shaves you probably work in a barber shop; a hair stylist might offer beard trims but is not set up with hot towels and other items associated with a professional barber shop shave.

If you use code 812112 it defines your profession as a hair stylist or beauty shop owner; these shops tend to cater to women, as well as men looking for a fashionable haircut.

If you run a beauty supply store you would use an entirely different business code, that number is 446120. A beauty supply store does not do hair; they sell hair care supplies. If you own both a salon and a supply store you have two separate businesses.

LINE C is left empty if you operate your business in your personal name. Otherwise fill in your business name here.

If you have obtained an EIN (Employer Identification Number), you can add this number on **LINE D**.

If you work out of your home leave **LINE E** empty. If you have an office address put it on this line.

Most independent business men and women operate on a CASH BASIS. That means you deduct an expense when it occurs, whether you pay in cash or get a bill, and count income the day it arrives in the mail.

The accrual system is complicated and used by larger businesses. Put an X in the cash box on **LINE F** unless you have an accountant, and then ask your accountant which system you use, it's probably cash.

LINE G is marked YES unless you do not participate in your own business, which is rare for a self-employed or independent business person.

LINE H is only checked on the first year that you operate your business. If this is your first Schedule C for this business check this box now. **LINE I** would be YES if you paid any one person more than $600 which would require the mailing of Form(s) 1099; **LINE J** would then also be checked yes if those forms were sent.

Now flip the form over and fill out the backside; the back of your Schedule C has to be filled out before you can continue with the front.

The top portion of the back, shown on the next page, begins with Part III – Cost of Goods Sold. This is where you will enter your inventory figures. If you do not have inventory skip Part III, and move on to Part IV of this form.

Schedule C (Form 1040) 2014   Page 2

Part III   **Cost of Goods Sold** (see instructions)

33	Method(s) used to value closing inventory: a ☐ Cost b ☐ Lower of cost or market c ☐ Other (attach explanation)	
34	Was there any change in determining quantities, costs, or valuations between opening and closing inventory? If "Yes," attach explanation . . . . ☐ Yes ☐ No	
35	Inventory at beginning of year. If different from last year's closing inventory, attach explanation	35
36	Purchases less cost of items withdrawn for personal use	36
37	Cost of labor. Do not include any amounts paid to yourself	37
38	Materials and supplies	38
39	Other costs	39
40	Add lines 35 through 39	40
41	Inventory at end of year	41
42	Cost of goods sold. Subtract line 41 from line 40. Enter the result here and on line 4 . . .	42

If you have inventory mark the first box on **LINE 33** with an X, showing that your inventory is valued at its cost.

If you valued it in a different manner last year check YES on **LINE 34**, otherwise mark the box marked NO.

Enter your beginning of the year inventory value on **LINE 35**; if you had no inventory at the start of the tax year put a zero in this box.

LINE 36 is where you enter the cost of all new inventory added during this tax year. You will find that figure by adding everything in Column 2 of the New Inventory Report you filled out earlier.

Labor, materials and supplies, and other expenses can be broken out and listed separately, but this is not required. Yours were added into inventory. Skipping Lines 37-39, write the number you posted on Line 36 onto **LINE 40**.

Going back to the New and Prior Year Inventory Reports in this book, add all the end of year inventory values together and place that total on **LINE 41**.

Subtract Line 41 from Line 40 and you will have the Cost of Goods Sold; enter this on **LINE 42**.

The back of the Schedule C also includes two sections titled Part IV - Information on Your Vehicle and Part V - Other Expenses. Those two sections are illustrated below.

If you use your personal vehicle, and only deduct mileage, you will need to fill out Part IV. The mileage deduction is generally more than $.50 per mile driven for business use, so even if you only drive a few miles on business errands it's well worth noting.

If you want to depreciate your vehicle, you are no longer preparing a simple Schedule C tax return. Depreciation is confusing, even for some tax professionals, and the rules change often. Depreciation instructions are not included in this guide.

If you are only taking the mileage deduction, on **LINE 43** write in the date that your vehicle was brought into your business and placed in service, even if this date is from a prior year.

If this is your primary employment you will not be allowed to deduct your commuting mileage. Getting to and from a person's primary job is not deductible.

Any mileage incurred in traveling from job one to job two is deductible, but going home after job two is not, unless it is farther from home than your primary job, then you can deduct those extra miles.

Enter all business miles on **LINE 44-a**, and all non-business miles, including non-deductible commute miles, on **LINE 44-b**.

Answer the questions on **LINES 45-47**. If you can't check the YES box on Line 47-b, you can't take a mileage deduction, so keep written records for all mileage.

Part V – OTHER EXPENSES is a catch-all section. Any expense that does not have a specific spot in Part II, on the front of the Schedule C, will be first listed here and then totaled and eventually posted to Line 27.

 If you have receipts in the expense envelopes labeled E-Education, G-Gifts, J-Job Related Licenses, N-Newspapers & Magazines, or S-Shipping, you will list each on a separate line here along with the total expense. Some education expenses may also qualify for education credits on your personal 1040; check current 1040 rules to see if this is a better option.

W-2 payroll expenses, but not actual wages distributed, will also be listed as Other Expenses. You'll need envelope "W" again later, but the others can be put into the "done" pile when you're finished.

Now let's go back to the front of your Schedule C, to Part I, and report your business income.

Part I	Income		
1	Gross receipts or sales. See instructions for line 1 and check the box if this income was reported to you on Form W-2 and the "Statutory employee" box on that form was checked . . . . ▶ ☐	1	
2	Returns and allowances	2	
3	Subtract line 2 from line 1	3	
4	Cost of goods sold (from line 42)	4	
5	**Gross profit.** Subtract line 4 from line 3	5	
6	Other income, including federal and state gasoline or fuel tax credit or refund (see instructions) . . .	6	
7	**Gross income.** Add lines 5 and 6 . . . . ▶	7	

On **LINE 1** enter all of your cash income - all money deposited into your bank accounts. This will include all 1099 income received.

If you refunded any money during the tax year, and this has not already been subtracted from your total income, enter that total on **LINE 2**.

Subtract Line 2 from Line 1 and enter this number on **LINE 3**; if you had no returns the number would be the same one that you entered on Line 1.

You have already completed the inventory section, Part III, on the back of this form. Transfer the number you wrote on Line 42, on the backside, to **LINE 4** on the front of your Schedule C.

Subtract Line 4 from Line 3 and write that number on **LINE 5**. If you had no inventory it will be the same as Line 3.

If you had barter income, rent office space or storage space to others, or had other income that you have not reported elsewhere in this section, or on your personal tax return, such as business interest income, bad debts claimed in prior years and recovered in this tax year, or equipment sold, enter that figure on **LINE 6**.

Add Line 5 and Line 6 together and write this number on **LINE 7**.

This is the Gross Income for your business. This is not your taxable business income; you must first subtract all expenses to arrive at that figure. So let's enter those business expenses in Part II.

The following illustration shows Part II of Schedule C.

Using Your Annual Tax Report you created post the rest of your expenses in Part II. Every expense total you were instructed to write on the front of the envelopes will be posted onto this portion of the form. Simply write the total from each envelope onto the matching line, unless instructed to include more information.

LINE 8 – A (Advertising & Promotional Expenses)

LINE 9 – V (Vehicle Car/Truck Expenses)

Taking the mileage deduction is easy. On the back of the Schedule C you simply fill out Part IV and multiply the total business miles that you entered on Line 44-a by the mileage rate allowed for the current tax year. For 2014 that rate was $.56 per mile. Enter this calculation on Line 9.

Car and truck expenses can be figured in two different ways. The first method is the mileage deduction which includes average depreciation, repairs and gas. You can choose instead to depreciate your vehicle and deduct exact expenses; you will need to fill out Form 4562 to use this method.

As stated earlier, depreciation is not simple, and therefore instructions for depreciation are not included in this guide. Depreciation is best left to the tax professionals and accounting majors.

LINE 10 – P (People Who Take a Share)

LINE 11 – W (Wages & Contract Labor Expenses) Only the Contract Labor portion belongs on Line 11 – other wage expenses are posted elsewhere.

LINE 12 – Leave this line empty as it is for reporting depletion of oil and gas fields.

Equipment with a longer life than one year must be listed on IRS Form 4562 before it can be deducted. Depreciation has to be tracked for the lifetime of the item, and has complicated rules; unless you have accounting training leave depreciation for the tax pros. Take the Section 179 option, it's easier.

If you have items in the Q envelope they will need to be entered on Form 4562 before you can take the Section 179 deduction. You will need to refer to Form 4562 instructions for other methods of depreciation.

Stop and fill out form 4562 now. You will find the instructions on page 80.

Once you have completed Form 4562 the amount at the bottom of that form, on Line 22, is transferred to **LINE 13** on your Schedule C.

LINE 14 – W (Wages & Contract Labor Expenses) If you have W-2 employees, and you offer benefit programs such as pension or daycare, you would list those expenses on Line 14.

LINE 15 – I (Insurance)

LINE 16 a-b - B (Bank, Visa & Other Business Interest)

If you are purchasing a building for your business the mortgage interest belongs on **LINE 16-a**; all other business interest belongs on **LINE 16-b**.

LINE 17 – L (Legal & Professional Fees)

LINE 18 – O (Office Supplies)

LINE 19 – If you have a pension or profit-sharing plan the dollar figure for Line 19 will be supplied by your plan administrator; a personal IRA deposit is posted to your 1040 personal tax return.

LINE 20 a-b – R (Rent Paid) Rental of office equipment, furniture or tools belongs on **LINE 20-a**; if you pay space rent that amount belongs on **LINE 20-b**.

LINE 21 – F (Fix-it & Repair Expenses)

LINE 22 – C (Cleaning Materials & Business Supplies)

LINE 23 – X (Taxes & Business Licenses)

LINE 24 a-b – T (Travel) and M (Meals & Entertainment)

Everything business travel related belongs on **LINE 24a**. All meals, even those during extended business travel, are totaled as one amount. You can deduct 50% of meal and entertainment expenses; before entering the total divide by two and put that number on **LINE 24-b**.

LINE 25 – U (Utilities) If you do not have a home office, but pay utilities for your business or office space, this expense will go on LINE 25.

LINE 26 – W (Wages & Contract Labor Expenses) Payroll wages are entered on Line 26.

LINE 27 is for all other expenses. Other Expenses include those in envelope E-Educational Seminars & Classes, G-Gifts, J-Job Required Licenses & Dues, N-Newspapers, Magazines & Subscriptions, S-Shipping & Postage, and any other miscellaneous expenses that could not be lumped into one of the other categories.

All of these items are first listed individually on the back of your Schedule C, under Part V - Other Expenses. Once they are itemized on the back, the grand total is then posted to Line 27. Do not include home office expenses; those are dealt with in another place.

Now that all of the expenses have been posted in Part II, you will total those expenses together and enter them on the final section on the front of your Schedule C. That section is shown below.

28	Total expenses before expenses for business use of home. Add lines 8 through 27a ▶	28		
29	Tentative profit or (loss). Subtract line 28 from line 7	29		
30	Expenses for business use of your home. Do not report these expenses elsewhere. Attach Form 8829 unless using the simplified method (see instructions). Simplified method filers only: enter the total square footage of: (a) your home: _____ and (b) the part of your home used for business: _____ . Use the Simplified Method Worksheet in the instructions to figure the amount to enter on line 30	30		
31	Net profit or (loss). Subtract line 30 from line 29. • If a profit, enter on both Form 1040, line 12 (or Form 1040NR, line 13) and on Schedule SE, line 2. (If you checked the box on line 1, see instructions). Estates and trusts, enter on Form 1041, line 3. • If a loss, you must go to line 32.	31		
32	If you have a loss, check the box that describes your investment in this activity (see instructions). • If you checked 32a, enter the loss on both Form 1040, line 12, (or Form 1040NR, line 13) and on Schedule SE, line 2. (If you checked the box on line 1, see the line 31 instructions). Estates and trusts, enter on Form 1041, line 3. • If you checked 32b, you must attach Form 6198. Your loss may be limited.	32a ☐ All investment is at risk. 32b ☐ Some investment is not at risk.		

For Paperwork Reduction Act Notice, see the separate instructions.   Cat. No. 11334P   Schedule C (Form 1040) 2014

Begin by adding Lines 8 thru 27, your expenses in Part II, and write that total on **LINE 28**.

Subtract Line 28 from Line 7 and enter that number on **LINE 29**.

This is your tentative profit or loss. However, if you have a home office you must complete one more step before you have the final figure.

You will need to fill out Form 8829 to take the home office deduction. Stop and fill out Form 8829 now. You will find instructions on page 84.

After filling out Form 8829, return here and enter the number you put on Line 35 of Form 8829 onto your Schedule C's **LINE 30**.

Subtract Line 30 from Line 29 and enter this number on **LINE 31**. If you had a loss, that number will have a minus (-) in front of it.

If you have a loss, but are working to create profit, check **BOX 32a**; otherwise mark **BOX 32b**. If you check Box 32b your loss will be limited.

If you do not have a home office or major equipment purchases, or you have already completed Form 4562 (Depreciation) and/or Form 8829 (Home Office), you're ready to finish the job. Instructions for Form 4562 follow; those for Form 8829 appear on page 82.

Now turn to page 86, the section on Posting Profit or Loss to your 1040 Tax Return, and let's finish your self-employment taxes.

Figuring Section 179 Deductions – Form 4562

Form 4562 is used when you have purchased items for your business that have an expected life of two or more years. The IRS requires that you track these items, and if they are sold before an item's depreciable life is over, you have to repay any undeserved depreciation that you have taken.

The only part of Form 4562 covered in these instructions is Section 179 deductions. A Section 179 deduction is when you take the entire cost of the item in the year of purchase. Each year a maximum amount is established for businesses using the Section 179 deduction. The maximum amount allowed for 2011 is $500,000.

Let's start by filling out the top portion. You'll find a copy of Form 4562 Part I below.

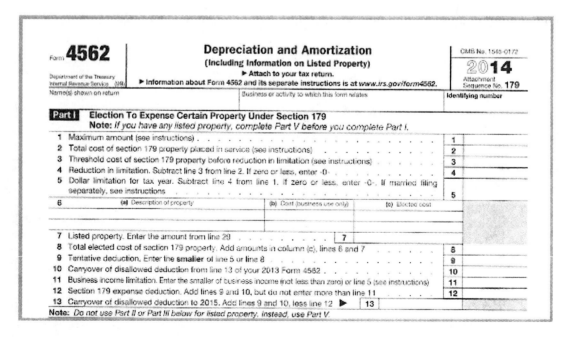

For 2014 taxes, write $500,000 on **LINE 1**. For any other years check the IRS Form 4562 instructions for the current figure.

On **LINE 2** write the total you posted to the front of your "Q" Equipment envelope.

No one with more than the maximum amount allowed for Section 179 deductions should be preparing their own taxes. Therefore **LINE 3** will be the same as Line 2. If this amount exceeds the current maximum, you are filing Married Filing Separately, or you sell a depreciated or Section 179 item, get guidance from a tax pro.

Everyone else will simply list the items purchased on **LINE 6**, writing the value of each item in both Column (b) and Column (c).

Leave **LINE 7** empty unless you are depreciating your vehicle; if you are doing this refer to Form 4562 Instructions.

LINE 8 is the equipment total from Column (c) plus Line 7. The smaller of Line 5 or Line 8 is then written on **LINE 9**. If you had a carryover of disallowed deductions on last year's return enter that number on **LINE 10**.

Unless you made more than the Section 179 maximum for that tax year, which will be printed in the current year's 4562 IRS instruction book, enter your business income from Schedule C Line 7 onto Form 4562 **LINE 11**.

Add Lines 9 and 10 together. If this amount is larger than Line 11, enter that figure on **LINE 12**; otherwise enter the total of Lines 9 and 10. Subtract Line 12, and enter this amount on **LINE 13**.

If you are depreciating other items use the IRS instruction book to complete Part II, Part III, Part V and Part VI of Form 4562. Complete these sections before following the instructions for completing the Summary at the bottom of the front of Form 4562.

If you completed Part V - Listed Property, transfer the number you put on Line 28 to **LINE 21**.

If you did not complete Parts II or III the figure on **LINE 22** will be the total of Line 21 plus Line 12. Otherwise, you will need to add lines 12, 14-17, 19 and 20(g) to Line 21 and put this figure on Line 22.

Unless you are subject to Uniform Capitalization Rules you will enter nothing on **LINE 23**.

Return to page 77 to learn where to post the number you just put on Line 22 of Form 4562. After that is done continue with the Schedule C instructions.

Taking the Home Office Deduction – Form 8829

Start by filling out the top of IRS Form 8829 – Expenses for Business Use of Your Home. This form can be downloaded at www.IRS.gov, by clicking on the link to Forms and Publications, and then on the link for Form 8829.

The top portion of Form 8829 begins by asking for the small business owner's name and social security number.

Part I is where you must provide details on the portion of your home that is used exclusively for your business on a regular basis. Earlier you gathered information on the square footage of your home and office plus expenses for your home office deductions. This information will now be entered in Part I of form 8829 as follows.

On **LINE** 1 enter the office square footage; the total square footage of your home goes on **LINE** 2. Divide Line 1 by Line 2 to get the percentage of your home that is set aside for business use and enter that number on **LINE** 3. You don't need Lines 4-6, they are for daycare facilities. Repeat the number you wrote on Line 3 on **LINE** 7.

Next, you will figure the allowable deduction by using Part II. The rest of the expenses that you posted on your Home Office Deductions sheet will be entered here.

Part II	Figure Your Allowable Deduction				
8	Enter the amount from Schedule C, line 29, **plus** any gain derived from the business use of your home, minus any loss from the trade or business not derived from the business use of your home (see instructions) See instructions for columns (a) and (b) before completing lines 9-21.				8
			(a) Direct expenses	(b) Indirect expenses	
9	Casualty losses (see instructions)	9			
10	Deductible mortgage interest (see instructions)	10			
11	Real estate taxes (see instructions)	11			
12	Add lines 9, 10, and 11	12			
13	Multiply line 12, column (b) by line 7			13	
14	Add line 12, column (a) and line 13				14
15	Subtract line 14 from line 8. If zero or less, enter -0-				15
16	Excess mortgage interest (see instructions)	16			
17	Insurance	17			
18	Rent	18			
19	Repairs and maintenance	19			
20	Utilities	20			
21	Other expenses (see instructions)	21			
22	Add lines 16 through 21	22			
23	Multiply line 22, column (b) by line 7		23		
24	Carryover of prior year operating expenses (see instructions)		24		
25	Add line 22, column (a), line 23, and line 24				25
26	Allowable operating expenses. Enter the **smaller** of line 15 or line 25				26
27	Limit on excess casualty losses and depreciation. Subtract line 26 from line 15				27
28	Excess casualty losses (see instructions)		28		
29	Depreciation of your home from line 41 below		29		
30	Carryover of prior year excess casualty losses and depreciation (see instructions)		30		
31	Add lines 28 through 30				31
32	Allowable excess casualty losses and depreciation. Enter the **smaller** of line 27 or line 31				32
33	Add lines 14, 26, and 32				33
34	Casualty loss portion, if any, from lines 14 and 32. Carry amount to **Form 4684** (see instructions)				34
35	**Allowable expenses for business use of your home.** Subtract line 34 from line 33. Enter here and on Schedule C, line 30. If your home was used for more than one business, see instructions ▶				35

Begin by entering the Tentative Profit or Loss from Line 29 of your Schedule C onto **LINE** 8 of Form 8829.

Because the figures that you entered on the forms in this book were for the entire house, all expenses will be entered in column (b) - Indirect Expenses. If you have any expenses on Lines 18-21 that were 100% business, such as a repair to the office ceiling, this would go into column (a) - Direct Expenses.

LINE 9 is only filled in if you had casualty losses.

Enter all of the mortgage interest from your 1099 on **LINE** 10.

Residence real estate taxes that were paid go on **LINE 11**.

Add Lines 9, 10 and 11 together and put that total on **LINE 12**.

Multiply Line 12 by the percentage you wrote on Line 7 of this form, and enter that figure on **LINE 13**. Anything leftover will end up on your personal Schedule A.

LINE 14 will be the total of Lines 12 and 13.

When you subtract Line 14 from Line 8, and enter that on **LINE 15**, you will know you how much of your mortgage interest and real estate taxes belong on your personal Schedule A.

The rest of your household expenses are reported as follows: Report your insurance on **LINE 17**, rent on **LINE 18**, home repairs and lawn maintenance on **LINE 19**, utilities on **LINE 20**, and any other expenses on **LINE 21**. Post any of these expenses that are 100% business related in Column (a); all others will go in Column (b). Add all of the numbers together from Column (b), and write that total on **LINE 22**.

Multiply Line 22 x Line 7 and write this number on **LINE 23**.

If you have any prior year operating carryovers, transfer that figure from last year's tax return to **LINE 24**.

Add Column (a) Line 22 to Lines 23 and 24 and write the total on **LINE 25**.

Compare Line 25 to Line 15 and write the smaller number on **LINE 26**.

Subtract Line 26 from Line 15 and enter that number on **LINE 27**.

If you had any casualty losses on Line 9, multiply any losses in excess of the amount listed by the percentage you wrote on Line 7 and enter the results on **LINE 28**.

You will have to complete Parts III and IV of this form before you can fill in the next two lines. Follow the directions below to complete Parts III and IV.

Depreciation of Your Home requires current basis figures. Your home's basis is the original cost of the home plus all updates made to your home, that have not already been depreciated. Compare your basis to the home's current fair market value and enter the smaller figure on **LINE 36**.

Part III	Depreciation of Your Home			
36	Enter the **smaller** of your home's adjusted basis or its fair market value (see instructions)	36		
37	Value of land included on line 36	37		
38	Basis of building. Subtract line 37 from line 36	38		
39	Business basis of building. Multiply line 38 by line 7	39		
40	Depreciation percentage (see instructions)	40		%
41	Depreciation allowable (see instructions). Multiply line 39 by line 40. Enter here and on line 29 above	41		
Part IV	Carryover of Unallowed Expenses to 2015			
42	Operating expenses. Subtract line 26 from line 25. If less than zero, enter -0-	42		
43	Excess casualty losses and depreciation. Subtract line 32 from line 31. If less than zero, enter -0-	43		

For Paperwork Reduction Act Notice, see your tax return instructions.　　Cat. No. 13232M　　Form **8829** (2014)

You will find the value assigned to your land on the last property tax statement received. Write that on **LINE 37**. Subtract Line 37 from Line 36 and enter that on **LINE 38**. Multiply Line 38 x Line 7 and enter this on **LINE 39**.

If you used your office for the entire year in 2011 write 0.107 on **LINE 40**. If you used it for less than a year, or this is a different tax year, you will need to look up the number for Line 40; it varies based on the first month of use and can be found in the current IRS Form 8829 Instructions at www.IRS.gov.

Multiply Line 7 x Line 40 and write this on **LINE 41**. Improvements made after the initial year of home office deductions require detailed entries on Form 4562. If you have new improvements, yours is no longer a simple tax return and a visit to a tax professional is advised. Enter the number you wrote on Line 41 on **LINE 29** in Part II.

You have to fill out Part IV before you can continue; it has only two lines. To fill in the first box you need to refer to Part II of this form. Subtract Line 26 from Line 25 in Part II, and enter this number on **LINE 42**.

Subtract Line 32 from Line 31 and enter this number on **LINE 43**, unless it is less than zero, then enter zero. Now you can finish Part II; take the number you wrote on Line 43 and transfer it to **LINE 30**.

Add Lines 28, 29 and 30 and enter the total on **LINE 31**. Compare Lines 27 and 31; write the smaller figure on **LINE 32**. Add Lines 14, 26 and 32 and write the sum on **LINE 33**.

If you are required to fill out Form 4684 due to casualty losses you'll need to fill in **LINE 34**, otherwise leave it blank. Subtract Line 34 from Line 33 and enter this on **LINE 35**. You will also need to enter this figure on your Schedule C tax form.

Return to page 79 for instructions on where to enter this figure on your Schedule C, and follow the rest of the instructions for completing your Schedule C tax return. When done come back to this page for help with the business portion of your 1040.

Posting Profit or Loss to your 1040 Tax Return

You cannot use tax form 1040EZ or 1040A for your personal taxes when you have Schedule C income; there is nowhere to include business income on those forms. You must use Form 1040. The portion you are concerned with appears below.

Income	7	Wages, salaries, tips, etc. Attach Form(s) W-2		7
	8a	Taxable interest. Attach Schedule B if required		8a
Attach Form(s) W-2 here. Also attach Forms W-2G and 1099-R if tax was withheld.	b	Tax-exempt interest. Do not include on line 8a	8b	
	9a	Ordinary dividends. Attach Schedule B if required		9a
	b	Qualified dividends	9b	
	10	Taxable refunds, credits, or offsets of state and local income taxes		10
	11	Alimony received		11
	12	Business income or (loss). Attach Schedule C or C-EZ		12
If you did not get a W-2, see instructions.	13	Capital gain or (loss). Attach Schedule D if required. If not required, check here ▶ ☐		13
	14	Other gains or (losses). Attach Form 4797		14
	15a	IRA distributions 15a	b Taxable amount	15b
	16a	Pensions and annuities 16a	b Taxable amount	16b
	17	Rental real estate, royalties, partnerships, S corporations, trusts, etc. Attach Schedule E		17
	18	Farm income or (loss). Attach Schedule F		18
	19	Unemployment compensation		19
	20a	Social security benefits 20a	b Taxable amount	20b
	21	Other income. List type and amount		21
	22	Combine the amounts in the far right column for lines 7 through 21. This is your **total income** ▶		22
Adjusted Gross Income	23	Educator expenses	23	
	24	Certain business expenses of reservists, performing artists, and fee-basis government officials. Attach Form 2106 or 2106-EZ	24	
	25	Health savings account deduction. Attach Form 8889	25	
	26	Moving expenses. Attach Form 3903	26	
	27	Deductible part of self-employment tax. Attach Schedule SE	27	
	28	Self-employed SEP, SIMPLE, and qualified plans	28	
	29	Self-employed health insurance deduction	29	
	30	Penalty on early withdrawal of savings	30	
	31a	Alimony paid b Recipient's SSN ▶	31a	
	32	IRA deduction	32	
	33	Student loan interest deduction	33	
	34	Tuition and fees. Attach Form 8917	34	
	35	Domestic production activities deduction. Attach Form 8903	35	
	36	Add lines 23 through 35		36
	37	Subtract line 36 from line 22. This is your **adjusted gross income** ▶		37

For Disclosure, Privacy Act, and Paperwork Reduction Act Notice, see separate instructions.   Cat. No. 11320B   Form **1040** (2014)

LINE 12, on the front page of the 1040, is where you post your business profit or loss. If you have a loss your number needs to have a minus in front of it. When you total all other income sources, on your 1040 personal tax form, an owner who is active in their business will subtract a loss from the total income that gets entered on **LINE 22.**

A Schedule C business loss (by an active owner) can reduce taxes on other earned income; passive income losses can only be offset by passive gains. SE Taxes, SE Health Insurance and Retirement Deposits are all business expenses which are deducted on your personal 1040.

You have already posted your business income or loss to Line 12, but you could have a few more business deductions. This guide does not explain how to complete a personal 1040 Tax Return, but for information on where to post other business expenses, those deducted on Form 1040.

If you had net earnings of more than $400 from self-employment you will need to fill out a Schedule SE to figure your Self-Employment Taxes before you can finish your personal 1040. Without that number you can't fill in lines 27 and 56.

Calculating Self-Employment Taxes

IRS Schedule SE is used to calculate self employment tax, otherwise known as Social Security and Medicare taxes. Let's start with the top of Schedule SE.

At the very top of the form there is a place for the name of the self-employed person and their social security number. This is followed by a series of simple questions to help you determine whether or not you need to fill out the back of the form.

Self-employed people with church employee income, and those who want to use the optional method for figuring income, must use the back of this form.

People with total earnings of more than $106,800, unreported tips, or who reported wages on Form 8919 for uncollected Social Security and Medicare Taxes, will also need to complete the back of this form.

Follow the form instructions or get help from a tax professional if you are required to fill out the back of Schedule SE. Everyone else can skip to the bottom of the front page and answer the six questions found there. The illustration on the following page shows the lower portion of this form so you can follow along.

LINE 1 is for farmers. Leave it blank. Post the net profit or loss from Line 31 of your Schedule C tax form to **LINE 2** of your Schedule SE.

1a	Net farm profit or (loss) from Schedule F, line 34, and farm partnerships, Schedule K-1 (Form 1065), box 14, code A	1a	
b	If you received social security retirement or disability benefits, enter the amount of Conservation Reserve Program payments included on Schedule F, line 4b, or listed on Schedule K-1 (Form 1065), box 20, code Z	1b	( )
2	Net profit or (loss) from Schedule C, line 31; Schedule C-EZ, line 3; Schedule K-1 (Form 1065), box 14, code A (other than farming); and Schedule K-1 (Form 1065-B), box 9, code J1. Ministers and members of religious orders, see instructions for types of income to report on this line. See instructions for other income to report	2	
3	Combine lines 1a, 1b, and 2	3	
4	Multiply line 3 by 92.35% (.9235). If less than $400, you do not owe self-employment tax; do not file this schedule unless you have an amount on line 1b . . . . ▶	4	
	Note. If line 4 is less than $400 due to Conservation Reserve Program payments on line 1b, see instructions.		
5	**Self-employment tax.** If the amount on line 4 is:		
	• $117,000 or less, multiply line 4 by 15.3% (.153). Enter the result here and on **Form 1040, line 57,** or **Form 1040NR, line 55**		
	• More than $117,000, multiply line 4 by 2.9% (.029). Then, add $14,508 to the result. Enter the total here and on **Form 1040, line 57, or Form 1040NR, line 55**	5	
6	**Deduction for one-half of self-employment tax.** Multiply line 5 by 50% (.50). Enter the result here and on **Form 1040, line 27, or Form 1040NR, line 27** 6		

For Paperwork Reduction Act Notice, see your tax return instructions. Cat. No. 11358Z Schedule SE (Form 1040) 2014

LINE 3 is the total of Lines 1 and 2, minus your self-employed health insurance deduction from Line 29 of your 1040. Multiply Line 3 by .9235 and enter this on **LINE 4**. If this amount is less than $400 you do not owe any self-employment tax and do not need to file this schedule, unless you have an amount on Line 1b.

If Line 4 is $106,800 or less, multiply this number by .153, and enter that total on **LINE 5**. If it is more than $106,800 multiply the number by .029, add $13,243.20 to the result, and enter that figure on Line 5 instead.

The number on Line 5 must also be entered on **LINE 56 ON THE BACK OF YOUR PERSONAL 1040.**

LINE 6 is half of Line 5. That number must also be entered on **LINE 27 ON THE FRONT OF YOUR PERSONAL 1040.** That completes the instructions for the self-employment tax form.

A married couple operating a small business together can choose which person's Social Security and Medicare account gets the credit. They may choose to split the business income in any manner they want. Simply complete two Schedule SE forms, one in each name when splitting. Combined, the two forms would equal all of the Schedule C profit.

Other 1040 Deductions

Besides lines 12, 27 and 56, where you entered your Schedule C income or loss and Self-Employment Taxes, your 1040 personal tax form has a few additional lines where you can take advantage of small business deductions.

You will find an illustration below showing the bottom of the front page of the 1040 tax form. This is where you will be making your entries.

Begin by entering your net business income from your Schedule C on line 12. Don't forget to put a minus (-) in front of the number if it is a loss, and to subtract it when totaling your annual income.

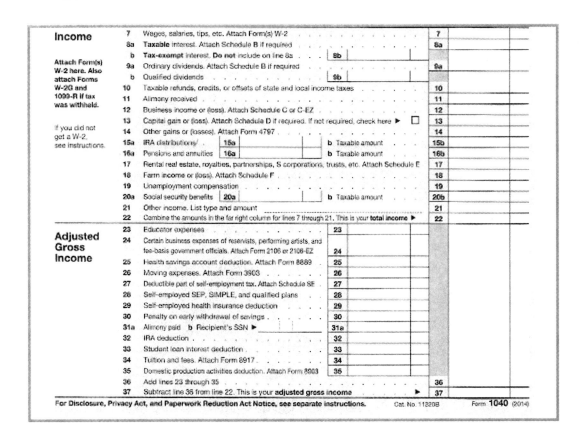

LINE 28 on your personal 1040 is where you will report any self-employed personal retirement plan contributions. Self-employed health insurance expenses are reported on LINE 29.

Follow the instructions for IRS Form 1040 for these two deductions. Each has its own personal 1040 requirements that may include additional tax forms. You will find rules and instructions for both of these in the IRS 1040 instruction book, or go online to www.IRS.gov.

There is one more line on your 1040, **LINE 35**, where a small business can enter their domestic production activities deduction. In order to have domestic production your small business would need to have at least one W-2 employee, produce products sold within the US, and fill out a complicated form. If your business is big enough to benefit from this deduction you will need to see a tax professional for help.

Finishing the Job

You are now ready to complete the rest of your personal 1040 tax return using the IRS 1040 Instruction Book. Fill it out just like you did in years prior to operating a business, adding business income and deductions as instructed. If having a small business makes it too confusing, take everything to a tax professional.

Anyone expecting to owe $1,000 or more in taxes for the following year is required to make estimated payments. These payments are based on the current year's taxable income and also referred to as Estimated Quarterly Tax Payments. As long as you pay in at least 100% of the taxes owed in the prior year, during the current tax year, you won't get hit with a penalty based on current laws.

Postmark your tax return and any payment due by April 15th and get a receipt when you put it in the mail.

The following chapter explains what to do with all of the papers you've collected. Keeping them is crucial to surviving an IRS tax audit.

DEVELOPING AN AUDIT-PROOF MINDSET

Establishing an audit-proof mindset is simple. When all income and expenses for a business are kept separate from personal funds, and every income and expense has a paper trail, you almost always survive a tax audit.

The exception comes when you have misinterpreted tax law. That's where the tax professional can help. If you're doing your own taxes, visiting a good tax accountant every 3-4 years for a heads-up on tax law changes, as well as any time life or business circumstances change, will keep you informed on current laws and help you to pay less tax.

Tax Pro Rule #10

**Without receipts you will fail a tax audit.
Box or bag your tax receipts and
keep those records for at least 6 years.
Copies of tax returns should be kept
a minimum of 10 years.**

Storage of tax records doesn't have to be fancy -- simply use a 1-2 gallon plastic food storage bag. Put the entire year's worth of expense envelopes and other information inside, write the tax year on the bag in indelible ink, and place that bag into a cardboard file box.

If you have lots of receipts you can store each year's receipts in a shoebox labeled with the tax year. There is no need to sort those receipts unless you are called for an audit.

Label a big storage box Tax Receipts -- this box needs to be large enough to hold 6-10 giant Ziploc bags or shoeboxes, each filled with a year's worth of receipts. When this storage box is full file it away and start a new box. If those records are older than 10 years remove and shred the oldest to make room for the current year.

Never store the only copy of your tax return or W-2's in this box. You will need a copy of your tax return and its accompanying W-2's if you apply for a mortgage or loan, so store them in a more convenient place. Keeping your tax return easily accessible will make filling out those applications easier.

The tax report forms you filled out in this book will be useful too, so don't hide this book away either. Those figures can be useful when writing a business plan or making inventory projections. Store this book with your other business financial information.

An IRS audit may sound scary, but an audit is nothing more than a meeting where the taxpayer is expected to show the receipts that back up the numbers he or she put onto a particular year's tax return. The person who has receipts is done quickly. But, because individuals are extremely likely to say too much during an audit, exposing other issues and causing the IRS to ask for more meetings and receipts, it's always smart to hire a tax accountant who specializes in audits to attend that meeting for you.

If you have a regular tax professional call him or her the day you receive that audit letter; dealing with audits on the returns they prepared is part of a tax professional's service. And, those tax professionals can represent you for any other tax audits as well, including those on tax returns that you prepared yourself.

Take your bag of receipt envelopes for the tax year being audited with you when you meet with that tax professional. He or she will know which papers will be needed to win the audit, and if you've followed all of the Tax Pro Rules those receipts will be in that bag and easy to find.

Planning for the Future

Many independent business people never move beyond the *Annual Tax Mess Organizer's* method of dealing with the annual chore of preparing information for their tax return. It may work well for the business owner with a small stack of expense receipts as well as self-employed people who hate doing paperwork, since they only have to tackle the job once a year.

To make life easier for tax procrastinators we now publish an *Annual Tax Mess Organizer 3-Year Form Book*. It includes copies of the same recordkeeping forms included in this book, enough for three separate tax years. Because you are already familiar with these forms, and know how to make short work out of sorting your records at tax time, you can expect to cut your time in half next year by using this book.

However, if you would like to learn how to get your financial records organized on a more regular basis, and how to use that same financial information that you gathered for your tax return to increase your profits you might want to try *30 Minutes to a Better Business: A Monthly Financial Organizer for the Self-Employed* next year.

This organizer can be used monthly, quarterly or semi-annually to track business income and expenses, and uses the same simple ABC method taught in this organizer. It includes all of the forms necessary for posting small business income and expenses monthly, tracking new and prior year inventory, and creating an annual tax report for your tax preparer. Plus, it teaches you how to use that information to figure out what is and is not working, so that you can improve your bottom line.

If you do not prepare your own tax return *Do My Business Taxes Please: A Financial Organizer for Self-Employed Individuals & Their Tax Preparers* may be the perfect choice for your future tax years.

It too includes all of the forms you will need to post your income and expenses on a regular basis, track inventory properly, create your annual tax report, and it uses the same simple ABC system. This book also has lots of help for entrepreneurs and small business owners who are working with a tax accountant.

Getting a Jump on the Next Tax Year

You'll want to start the new tax year with a fresh mileage log in every vehicle that you use within your business, as well as an envelope for stashing loose receipts and a small spiral notepad so that you can create your own receipts when one is not available.

Switching to a fresh checkbook register for the new tax year will make it easy to keep each year's tax records separate. When you do this it allows you to store your old checkbook register right along with your other tax receipts and records. This is handy if you're ever audited.

You will also want to start fresh folders or envelopes at your office and home for expense receipts too. It's important to keep each tax year's receipts separate in case of an audit.

If you have any remaining inventory on your shelves at the close of the tax year you'll want to get your new organizer right away because you're going to need a Prior Year Inventory Report to track that inventory for next year's tax return.

And, if you'll be adding new inventory soon you'll need a New Inventory Report too. Now is the time to start both and they are contained in all of the tax organizers mentioned.

If you do run inventory keep your new tax organizer where you normally receive your business inventory shipments. This will make it easy to add new inventory items to that New Inventory Report the moment it arrives. Getting your organizer now will give you a big jump on next year's tax mess.

TAX PROFESSIONALS

Tax professionals provide help with tax returns all across the U.S., but not all are qualified to do more than fill out a simple 1040 personal return.

When selecting a new tax preparer never choose one based on his or her reputation for getting everybody huge refunds. Everyone's tax circumstances are different, even when they appear to be the same to a person who has no tax training. And besides, a lot of those large tax refunds would never survive a thorough IRS audit.

Before allowing someone to prepare your taxes, ask how many business tax returns they have prepared. If they have done less than 50 Schedule C returns go elsewhere; many seasonal tax offices allow first year preparers to do small business returns. Although this may be good training for the new preparer, it's a bad deal for you. Experience is what makes a tax professional good.

The federal government now has a licensing system for tax preparers; prior to that only two states required proof that preparers were qualified to prepare personal tax returns. California and Oregon have tested and licensed their tax preparers for decades.

Always ask about a tax preparer's experience and licenses before hiring them to do your taxes. All accountants are licensed, but you want a tax accountant, someone who specializes in small business tax returns.

Accountants know more about tax law than most seasonal preparers. However, a licensed tax preparer who specializes in Schedule C tax returns will often know just as much about small business tax returns.

Choose an accountant or tax professional who does tax returns for others in your line of business, and choose one that fits your budget. Get someone who teaches you how to pay less tax legally, and never hire someone who suggests you break the rules. Here's a quick recap of those ten tax pro rules.

Tax Pro Rule #1

Absolutely all business income, including all cash & tips, must be deposited into a separate checking account used only for business funds.

Tax Pro Rule #2

Every penny spent or charged for your business needs a paper trail. If a receipt is not provided, you can make your own.

Tax Pro Rule #3

Every business barter exchange requires a paper trail assigning value to your time, or the product you traded for another's time or product.

Tax Pro Rule #4

Sorting expense receipts is as easy as ABC when you use the business expense alphabet.

Tax Pro Rule #5

Any equipment purchased, with an expected life of two or more years must be depreciated or expensed as a Section 179 deduction.

Tax Pro Rule #6

Unless you have a vehicle used only for business keep a notebook in the car and write down every business mile.

Tax Pro Rule #7

All items purchased or created for resale are considered to be inventory by the IRS. Inventory expenses can only be deducted as that inventory is sold.

Tax Pro Rule #8

No matter how good your tax professional is, if you don't provide all of the necessary information and figures your tax return will be wrong.

Tax Pro Rule #9

Tax laws change every year, sometimes offering huge tax savings for only a short time. Even if you do your own taxes, it is wise to speak with a tax pro occasionally, just to keep up on new tax credits and tax planning opportunities.

Tax Pro Rule #10

Without receipts you will fail a tax audit. Box or bag your tax receipts and keep those records for at least 6 years. Copies of tax returns should be kept a minimum of 10 years.

INDEX

MORE TAX ORGANIZERS BY KIKI CANNIFF
FOR TAX PROCRASTINATORS

Annual Tax Mess Organizers are for independent contractors who don't like doing paperwork on a regular basis. It teaches you exactly what the IRS expects and makes it easy to get a whole year's worth of records organized all at once. The basic book will work for all industries; it uses explanations and examples that are broad-based and covers a variety of professions. Industry-specific organizers contain only industry-based examples. For those who already prepare their own income taxes there's even a chapter on how to fill out and file a Schedule C tax return.

Annual Tax Mess Organizer are available for:
Barbers, Hair Stylists & Salon Owners
Independent Building Trade Contractors
Massage Therapists, Estheticians & Spa Owners
Nail Techs, Manicurists & Salon Owners
Sales Consultants & Home Party Sales Reps
Self-Employed People & Independent Contractors (Basic Book)
The Cannabis/Marijuana Industry
Writers, Artists, Self-Publishers & Craftspeople

NEW! ANNUAL TAX MESS ORGANIZER 3-YEAR FORM BOOK for tax-time procrastinators who love the annual method. This book includes all of the forms found in the current Annual Tax Mess Organizer for tracking income, expenses, inventory and tax-time reporting --- enough for three complete tax years!

INDEPENDENT CONTRACTORS WORKING WITH TAX PROFESSIONALS

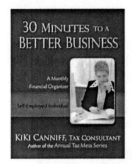

30 Minutes to a Better Business: A Monthly Financial Organizer for the Self-Employed is the perfect book for the independent contractor who wants to check their bottom line more often than once a year. It uses the same simple system taught in the Annual Tax Mess Organizers and includes all of the forms you need to track income and expenses monthly, track your inventory and compile the information you need for your annual tax return. Plus it teaches you how to use that information to improve your bottom line. No computer needed.

Do My Business Taxes Please; A Financial Organizer for Self-Employed Individuals and their Tax Preparers is a great organizational tool for people who use a tax professional. It will help you to know what you need and get organized for your tax appointment. Forms for documenting business income, expenses, and other tax-wise details are included, plus there's an annual tax report section for totaling and presenting those figures to your tax preparer. This book uses the same simple ABC method taught in the Annual Tax Mess Organizers.

Creativity is my Business; A Financial Organizer for Artists, Musicians, Photographers, Writers & Other Talented Individuals is for part-time and freelance creative individuals who want to avoid the IRS hobby classification. It explains IRS rules in simple terms, includes forms for tracking your work activities, explains how taxes affect freelancers in creative occupations, teaches creative people how to use tax laws to their benefit, and makes it easy to track business income, expenses & inventory, & to work with a preparer. No computer needed.

Gambling is my Business; A Financial Organizer for Professional Card Players & Other Gamblers is for professional gamblers who want to avoid the IRS hobby classification as well as the one-time big casino winner. It explains IRS tax rules as they pertain to gamblers, how a gambler can use business tax laws to their benefit, makes it easy to track gambling activities, income and expenses, and will help to keep you audit proof. This tax organizer makes it easy to get ready for your a tax preparer. No computer needed.

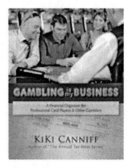

For more information visit www.OneMorePress.com